GREEN GUIDE

SEA SHELLS
AND OTHER
MARINE MOLLUSCS

·····························

OF AUSTRALIA

Nigel Marsh

First published in 2018 by Reed New Holland
Sydney

Level 1, 178 Fox Valley Road, Wahroonga, NSW 2076, Australia

newhollandpublishers.com

A record of this book is held at the British Library and the National Library of Australia.

ISBN 978 1 92151 799 0

Group Managing Director: Fiona Schultz
Publisher and Project Editor: Simon Papps
Designer: Andrew Davies
Production Director: James Mills-Hicks
Printed in China

10 9 8 7 6 5 4 3 2 1

Front cover:
Reaper Cuttlefish (main image),
mating Mourning Cuttlefish (top),
Common Pipis (left) and
Dimidiate Auger (bottom).

Photographic Acknowledgements
All images by Nigel Marsh.

Acknowledgement and Dedication
To Neville Coleman, Australia's greatest marine natural history author and educator,
and the first to published live images of Australian shells and molluscs in his classic
book *What Shell is That?* I am following in a giant's footsteps.

Keep up with New Holland Publishers:

 NewHollandPublishers
 @newhollandpublishers

CONTENTS

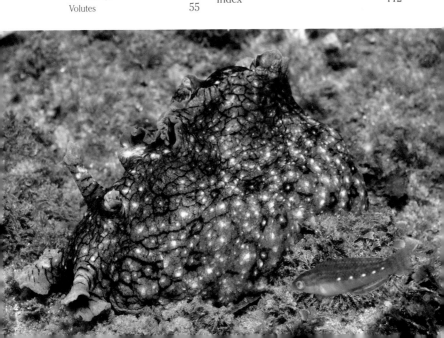

AN INTRODUCTION TO SEA SHELLS AND OTHER MARINE MOLLUSCS

Millions of sea shells wash up on beaches each year, a treasure trove of species for beachcombers to find.

Sea shells have always fascinated people, and have formed a part of human culture for thousands of years. While the soft-bodied creatures living within the shell is used for food, the shells themselves have been coveted by humans and used as jewellery, money and decoration.

Sea shells are part of the very large mollusc family, a collection of invertebrate species second only to the insects in number. The mollusc family not only contains the sea shells, but also the chitons, octopus, sea hares, nudibranchs, squid and cuttlefish. Most of these creatures look nothing like each other, but they all have similar body features that classify them as molluscs.

In this guide you will delve into the world of sea shells and marine molluscs and look at a range of wonderful species found around Australia. Designed for the diver, snorkeler and beachcomber, this book is a great introduction to anyone interested in sea shells and other marine molluscs.

This Lightning Volute shows many of the features of a typical mollusc, including an external shell, a large foot and a retractable proboscis.

Which Molluscs can be found in the Oceans?

The molluscs make up an extremely diverse group of invertebrates. They vary greatly in size, shape and behaviour. With more than 112,000 species contained in the family, this is the second largest group of animals on the planet. Molluscs are also the most predominant creatures found in the oceans, where they make up almost a quarter of all marine organisms. However, molluscs don't only live in ocean environments, as many species also live in freshwater rivers, lakes and on land.

Molluscs first evolved more than 500 million years, and for many millions of years they dominated the oceans. While they have changed greatly in size, shape and appearance over time, and many species have become extinct, the family today is split into seven classes. The gastropods are the largest class, containing 80 per cent of known mollusc species. Within this class are the sea shells, and all the snail and slug-like creatures. The bivalves are the second largest class, with this family containing molluscs with two shells, such as the clams, scallops and oysters. The chitons are a smaller mollusc class with overlapping armour-like shells. The cephalopods are the most advanced and intelligent of all the invertebrates, with this class containing the nautilus, squid, cuttlefish and octopus.

Species within these four classes are common around Australia and regularly encountered by divers, snorkelers and beachcombers. Less common, and not covered in this book, are the classes scaphopoda, or tusk shells, the monoplacaphora, or cap shells, and the aplacophora, which are worm-like molluscs without a shell.

Typical Mollusc features

There are several basic body characteristics that identify an animal as a mollusc. All these creatures have a body mantle which covers the organs and nervous system and is used for breathing and excretion. The mantle in most species secretes a hard calcium shell to protect the body, but some species have an internal shell, whilst others have no shell at all. The genitals and anus open directly into the mantle. Molluscs

Not all molluscs have external shells as the cuttlefish have an internal shell known as a cuttlebone.

also have an unsegmented and bilaterally symmetrical body. Another common molluscs feature is the radula – a rasp-like feeding tongue with serrated or ribbon-like teeth, which is used to break up food into digestible pieces. They also possess a

Molluscs vary greatly in form, with some of the prettiest being the colourful nudibranchs.

simple nervous-system structure, with two pairs of main nerve cords.

While these anatomical features are present in all molluscs, these animals vary so dramatically between classes that other characteristics are only common to each class or family. Most molluscs move with the aid of a large foot, which can also be used for digging for food or shelter. The cephalopods don't have a foot, and instead have arms and tentacles. Another common feature is the head, which contains sensory organs, a mouth and eyes. However, vision varies greatly between mollusc families, with some having good eyesight and others seeing only basic light and shadows. The hard external shell may seem like a common mollusc feature, but it varies so greatly in design, shape and purpose – if it is present at all – that it is not a universal characteristic of the molluscs.

Mollusc reproduction

Methods of reproduction in the mollusc family are almost as varied as the species, as some have separate sexes and others are hermaphrodites, having both male and female sexual organs. The genital openings in many species are located in the neck, however male cephalopods have a modified arm that acts like a penis to deliver sperm to the female.

Nudibranchs are hermaphrodites and have their sexual organs located in the neck, as can be seen in this mating pair.

A pair of Mourning Cuttlefish mating, locked together in a tangle of arms.

A few mollusc families reproduce using external fertilization, simply depositing eggs and sperm on the bottom of the ocean or releasing them into the water column. However, most species use internal fertilization. Mating molluscs either swap sperm if they are hermaphrodites, or the male inseminates the female. The young molluscs then develop in eggs, which are usually laid in clumps on the bottom, but some species keep their eggs inside their body cavity until they are ready to hatch. Many mollusc species die after

Each winter thousands of Giant Cuttlefish gather off Whyalla, South Australia, to mate and have become a major tourist attraction.

After mating, nudibranchs lay eggs in ribbon-like clumps.

reproducing and show no paternal bond with their young, however the protective female octopus guards her eggs until they hatch.

Most mollusc species have a larval stage that looks nothing like their adult form. Upon emerging from the egg, the larvae drift with ocean currents as a form of plankton. When large enough, the larvae descends to the seafloor and metamorphoses into its adult form. The cephalopods don't go through this process, as when they emerge from the egg they look like a miniature version of the adult.

Mollusc homes and habitats

Molluscs are found in all marine habitats from the shallows to the deep oceans. These diverse creatures have adapted to occupy every marine environment and are found in mangroves, mudflats, rock pools, coral reefs, rocky reefs and on sandy seafloors. While most mollusc species live on the bottom, some of these creatures also live a pelagic lifestyle, swimming in mid-water or drifting with ocean currents. While the squid are the most obvious of these ocean wanderers,

The Flashing File Shell lives in dark caves, keeping it safe from hungry fish.

numerous gastropod species also travel the oceans, using gas in their shells or body for flotation.

Some molluscs like to hide in the sand, like this stromb which has its eyes out looking for prey.

Although most molluscs live in saltwater, a number of species have adapted to live in freshwater, and are found in streams, rivers, ponds and lakes. You can even find molluscs on land, with numerous species of snails and slugs occupying a wide variety of environments, including backyard gardens.

Within their chosen habitat, most mollusc species like to hide during the day, as the great majority are nocturnal. Molluscs hide under rocks, coral, debris and many even disappear into the sand. But once the sun sets the molluscs emerge to feed and mate under the cover of darkness, when they are less likely to be eaten by other animals.

What do Molluscs eat?

Nudibranchs feed on many different foods. This pair of Papillate Armina are consuming a sea pen.

Molluscs vary greatly in their choice of food and how they catch and eat it. Many gastropods are grazers, consuming algae and seaweeds, but other members of this family scavenge on dead animals or capture prey to eat. Different members within this family eat very different prey. Cone shells eat fish they stun with a poisonous dart, while triton shells like to eat seastars (starfish). Other gastropods eat crustaceans, bacteria, worms, corals, anemones, sponges and even other molluscs. To consume their meal some gastropods swallow their prey whole, while others slowly rip it apart with their radula teeth, and some even slowly suck out their prey's insides.

Most bivalves, which are generally anchored to the bottom, are filter-feeders. These molluscs suck in great quantities

Egg Cowries are always found on soft corals, as this is their favourite food.

of water daily and collect phytoplankton on their gills. The gills are covered in hair-like filaments called cilia, which capture food particles and transport them to the mouth. Members of the chiton family are mostly grazers, stripping off algae with their strong radula teeth as they slowly move across rocks.

The cephalopods are all hunters, and feed on a variety of prey, including

Many molluscs eat other molluscs, such as this Baler Shell feeding on a Tiger Cowry.

crustaceans, fish and other molluscs. The squid and cuttlefish grab prey with their tentacles, while the octopus use their arms to trap prey. They then rip their food apart with their powerful parrot-like beaks. A number of cephalopods have a venomous bite that is used to immobilise prey and make them easier to consume.

Which Molluscs are dangerous?

The maps of ancient mariners used to depict sea monsters in unknown areas that hadn't been explored. Many of these sea monsters were shown as giant octopus and enormous squid, and while large species of these animals are potential dangerous

The Blue-lined Octopus is highly venomous, but fortunately docile and prefers to avoid people.

to divers, they have never sunk a ship or devoured sailors. However, the mollusc family does contain some dangerous members, and most of them are very small.

Most sea shells pose little danger to people, apart from sharp oysters cutting the feet of careless beachgoers or people suffering food poisoning from an off batch of mussels. In old movies giant clams were shown to trap divers by closing their shell on a leg, but this is just a myth as most giant clams cannot completely close their shells, let alone trap a diver. The most dangerous sea shells are members of the cone family that fire poisonous darts to stun their prey. The poison in these darts is also deadly to humans, and dozens of fatalities from cone venom have been recorded. Numerous cone shell species are found in the waters around Australia, so you are best advised not to touch any cone-like shell.

The blue-ringed octopus are also deadly members of the mollusc family. These small octopus have a venomous bite, which they use to stun prey, but have also killed a number of people. These octopus only bite people to defend themselves, when picked up or handled. They even have bright blue rings to warn other animals that they are venomous and to stay away. At least three species of blue-ringed octopus are found in the seas around Australia, and they are usually easy to avoid. It is thought that all octopus and cuttlefish have venomous bites, but in most species the venom is much weaker.

Old movies also used to depict giant octopus attacking and drowning divers. In reality large octopus are shy and avoid divers. However, occasionally one of these cephalopods shows interest in a diver and reaches out a curious and cautious arm to inspect the bubble-blowing alien visitor to its realm.

Cone shells fire venomous darts to stun their prey and should never be touched or handled.

Mollusc defences

Most molluscs have very succulent meat, which many people, and many animals, enjoy consuming. So these creatures have developed a number of defences to avoid becoming a meal. Gastropods and bivalves rely on their hard shells to protect them from predators. Unfortunately, this doesn't always work as many clever predators have evolved ways to either smash, bore, lever or crack open the shell. To avoid these predators, sea shells hide or camouflage themselves during the day, and many only emerge at night when fewer predators are active.

Nudibranchs are very colourful and easily spotted, but with distasteful flesh they are eaten by few predators.

Members of the heterobranch subclass don't have a hard shell to protect them from predators, so have developed other defences. Many of these creatures rely on camouflage for concealment, but others use chemical and biological weapons to defend themselves. Sea hares are good swimmers that will swim away from danger if possible, and to cover their escape they can squirt clouds of ink in a similar way to the cephalopods. A few nudibranchs can also swim away from predators, but most rely on their poisonous flesh to deter attack. However, a few members of this family have developed an ability to eat stinging hydroids and then store the stinging cells on their body for their own defence.

Cuttlefish use their cryptic camouflage skills to keep them hidden from predators.

The cephalopods also have soft bodies,

Most octopus stay safe from predators by hiding in a den.

with most species using camouflage and concealment to avoid being eaten. However, these clever creatures also deter predators by squirting ink, swimming rapidly and even sacrificing an arm to aid an escape. The octopus are very clever at avoiding predators, and have been known to fight back in order to scare off an attacker, and will even hang onto a predator until it gives up and swims off.

Life after death for Molluscs

People have always collected sea shells as trinkets and for decoration, however many animals also use old sea shells, giving these structures a second life after the death of the host. Hermit crabs rely on sea shells to protect their soft abdomens. Unlike other crabs, hermit crabs are not fully covered by a tough exoskeleton and have a soft underbelly. Hermit crabs have solved this problem by using old sea shells as a mobile home. As hermit crabs grow they have to upgrade to a new home, so are always on the lookout for vacant shells. However, some shells are so highly prized that hermit crabs fight over them or even pull other crabs out of them.

Hermit crabs are not the only animals that reuse old shells. Old shells are often used by small fish, worms, crustaceans and even other molluscs as places to hide or lay eggs. Another animal that recycles old shells is

Hermit crabs use old shells as a home and are always looking for an upgrade as they grow.

the Coconut Octopus (*Amphioctopus marginatus*). This octopus species is the only mollusc that is known to use tools, as they collect old bivalve shells to close around them for protection. If the octopus finds a good set of shells it will hold onto them, walking across the bottom with a firm grip on its prized mobile home.

Cuttlebones, found inside cuttlefish, also become a home to other creatures as they float on the surface and drift with ocean currents. Barnacles quickly attached to cuttlebones, but these floating rafts also become a home to small crabs and fish.

Mollusc associates and hitchhikers

The shells of molluscs are a solid surface that other animals and plants find ideal to attach to. Many sea shells get a covering of algae. The molluscs don't seem to mind this hairy growth, and it often has the benefit of providing camouflage. However, bigger sea shells also get larger growths, with sea anemones, sponges, sea weeds and corals growing on their exterior. These growths are not a problem for static bivalves such as clams and oysters, but for more mobile gastropods these growths can sometimes limit their mobility. Barnacles also frequently attach to sea shells, looking like a shell growing on a shell, but barnacles are actually a type of crustacean.

Small fish, crabs and shrimps also hide on larger sea shells, using them to shelter from other animals that might eat them. Recently it was discovered that Klein's Butterflyfish (*Chaetodon kleinii*) has a strange relationship with the Giant Clam (*Tridacna gigas*). The butterflyfish have been documented entering the clam via the siphon to clean the animal's gills, but may also enter the clam to hide from predators.

Some molluscs also get hitchhikers, with small worms and crustaceans using these creatures for a free ride. The most famous of these freeloaders is the Imperial Shrimp (*Periclimenes imperator*). These colourful shrimps make a home on several species of nudibranch, and get carried around like a member of the royal family on tour. Imperial Shrimps generally feed on algae and plankton, but will also feast on the faecal matter of their host.

Imperial Shrimps live on other animals, with this one hitchhiking on the tail end of a nudibranch.

Ancient Peoples and Molluscs

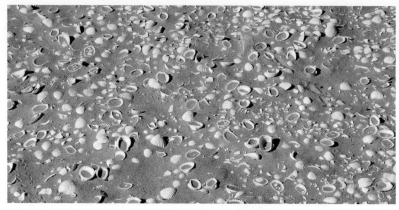

Piles of discarded shells consumed by Australian Aboriginals are known as middens.

Sea shells have been collected and used by almost every culture on Earth for many thousands of years. The colours and patterns of sea shells are hard to resist, and even today sea shells are collected by beachcombers. However, ancient people didn't just collected sea shells for display and decoration, as shellfish were also an important source of food.

Coastal peoples around the world have always gathered sea shells in the shallows for food. In Australia, sea shells were an important source of food for coastal Aboriginal and Torres Strait Islander people for thousands of years. Evidence of their importance is found in middens – large mounds of discarded shells – which can be several thousand years old. These middens are important archaeological sites, providing evidence about the diet of the local inhabitants over a long stretch of time. Middens are found around Australia at sites close to a good source of sea shells, like beaches, headlands, rock platforms and estuaries.

Shell fishhooks are commonly found in these middens. To catch fish, Aboriginals learnt to make fishhooks out of turban shells and other species. The shells were ground to shape on a stone until a C-shaped or J-shaped hook was created. A sharp hook was formed at one end by careful filing, and a notch at the other end so a line could be attached. Line was made from bark fibre or flax, and no bait was attached to the hook. Instead, cut up shellfish was chewed and spat on the surface near the hook, which with is shiny surface was an effective lure. These fishhooks were only used by women, the men preferring to spear their fish.

Fishhooks were not the only shell tool used by Aboriginals. They also used sharp shell edges like a knife for cutting meat and also in ceremonial rituals involving body markings or mutilations. Australian Aboriginals and Torres Strait Islanders also collected many species of sea shells to make decorative necklaces and headbands, which were typically used in ceremonies and sometimes for trade.

Other cultures around the world also collected sea shells for food and decoration, but these items also had many other uses. Cowry shells, one of the prettiest of all the shells, were once widely used as a form of currency throughout Asia and Africa. Abalone, pearl and other sea shells have also been used for many centuries to make buttons. In the Mediterranean, murex shells have been collected for many thousands of years to make a rich purple or blue dye. This dye was so expensive and exclusive that it was only used to dye the clothing worn by royalty and for religious ceremonies.

Should I collect shells?

Beachcombing is a popular activity at Australian beaches, and many pretty shells wash up each day with the tide.

People have collected sea shells for a very long time. While ancient people collected shells for food and body decoration, the Romans and Greeks also collected shells just for their beauty. While the average person today will collect sea shells they find on the beach, or buy one from a tourist shop, there are many serious shell collectors around the world, and some shells are worth a great deal of money. However there are many environmental issues associated with shell collecting.

The collection and study of sea shells is known as conchology. However, most shell collectors are not conchologists, as they are more interested in the beauty, rarity and value of the shell rather than studying it.

Most people start collecting shells by picking them up at the beach. This is generally not a problem in most locations, but in tropical areas where land hermit crabs are common, it can mean a housing crisis for the poor crabs. The major problem with shell collecting starts when people take them from the ocean, or buy them from shops or online.

Shells found underwater are generally in far better condition than those washed up on the beach, which often become chipped or scratched. If you do feel compelled to collect shells, you should of course only take dead shells, and never from marine reserves like the Great Barrier Reef. Even taking dead shells deprives hermit crabs and other species that rely on vacant shells as homes. Picking up dead shells doesn't

Shops often sell sea shells, which have unfortunately been collected live from the ocean.

come without risk, as around Australia these shells are often occupied by venomous blue-ringed octopus, which like to hide deep in the curls of the shell. Even though the risk of being bitten by a blue-ringed octopus is low, why risk death just to collect a pretty shell?

Buying shells from shops or online is not recommended. Most of these shells have been collected by divers on reefs across South-East Asia, and are generally taken while still alive. These delicate coral reef systems are already under pressure from climate change, aquarium collecting, coral collecting, coral bleaching, illegal fishing, dynamite fishing and many other practices. More marine reserves are required throughout South-East Asia in order to protect these important reefs and the molluscs and other creatures that live on them.

While many shell collectors are aware of environment issues associated with their hobby, many others don't care as rare shells are worth a great deal of money. However, the shell collecting market is so lucrative that many fake shells are often sold for a high price. These are not artificial shells, but shells that have been modified by polishing, bleaching, heating, painting or by some other process to make them look unique or like a new species.

If you want to see wonderful shell collections the best place to view them is a museum. Most natural history museums around Australia have a great display of shells. So next time you are beachcombing or snorkelling and find a nice shell, think before you pick it up – will it look nice on your bookcase gathering dust or would it make a great home for a hermit crab?

Avoid buying sea shells from shops, as reefs across South-East Asia have been plundered for these tourist trinkets.

Molluscs as seafood

Numerous mollusc species are consumed by humans every day. The most popular types eaten by people include oysters, scallops, mussels, abalone and squid. While a variety are taken by recreational fishers, commercial fishers heavily target many of these mollusc species around Australia. How these mollusc species are gathered varies greatly, as some are sustainably farmed through aquaculture, while others are harvested from the sea by trawlers, fishing boats and by hand.

SCALLOPS

In Australia around 2,100 tonnes of scallops are commercially harvested each year. Two species are taken for human consumption: the Southern Scallop (*Pecten fumatus*) and the Doughboy Scallop (*Chlamys asperrimus*). While divers can collect a limited number of scallops by hand, which has little impact on the marine environment, commercially they are trawled in Bass Strait using a scallop harvester. This is a net dragged across the sandy bottom, which destroys benthic life (bottom-dwelling marine life) and also catches other species as bycatch. This is easily the most destructive mollusc fishery in Australia.

SQUID

A smaller and more environmentally friendly Australian mollusc fishery is the Southern Squid Jig Fishery, which captures around 330 tonnes of squid annually. Captured at night from fishing boats rigged with lights and squid jigs, they generally target Gould's Squid (*Nototodarus gouldi*). These squid are mostly captured by boats

operating off the southern states. Recreational fishers also capture many squid, but more commonly jig for Southern Calamari Squid (*Sepioteuthis australis*) and Bigfin Reef Squid (*Sepioteuthis lessoniana*). As squid have a short lifespan, these fisheries are quite sustainable if managed properly.

ABALONE

Abalone is big business Down Under, and collected by both recreational and commercial divers. Recreational divers can only collected a limited number for their own personal consumption, while commercial divers are licensed to collect abalone and have to work within a quota system. Abalone diver licenses are worth millions of dollars, and with the high price of abalone meat the industry generates hundreds of millions of dollars

a year in revenue. Australia provides a third of the world's abalone supply, and most of this comes from Tasmania. Abalone is also collected in New South Wales, Victoria, South Australia and Western Australia.

In Australia four species of abalone are collected by divers: Greenlip Abalone (*Haliotis laevigata*), Blacklip Abalone (*Haliotis rubra*), Brownlip Abalone (*Haliotis conicopora*) and Roe's Abalone (*Haliotis roei*). Commercial divers generally work using hookah (surface supplied air) and collect thousands of abalone a day. It is a very hard job working long hours in cold water, and while the occasional Great White Shark (*Carcharodon carcharias*) is known to check out abalone divers, they face more risks from pressure-related injuries such as decompression sickness. Most abalone collected in Australia is exported to Asian markets, and with the high price of the meat there is also a thriving black market. While quotas are set to ensure that the industry is sustainable, the flourishing black market means that abalone numbers continue to decline. Recently, abalone farming has started in Australia, and hopefully this will safeguard the future population of these important molluscs.

OYSTERS

One of the most popular molluscs consumed by Australians is the oyster. The Aboriginals were first to feast on this delicacy, evidenced by the huge piles of oyster shells found in middens. The first European settlers also ate many oysters and used their shells for lime production. They eventually stripped

the natural oyster beds bare, and then turned to farming them, creating the first aquaculture industry in the late 1800s. Today three species of oysters are farmed in Australia: Sydney Rock Oyster (*Saccostrea glomerata*), Flat Oyster (*Ostrea angasi*) and Pacific Oyster (*Crassostrea gigas*).

Oysters are now farmed in New South Wales, Queensland, Tasmania and Western Australia. Around 170 million oysters are harvested annually. Oyster farms are generally located in tidal estuaries, and are basically timber structures that give oysters a solid base upon which to grow. Although oyster farming is sustainable, water quality is always an issue as these bivalves are filter-feeders and can't tolerate pollution fouling their water. Oyster farmers around Australia are always fighting to ensure that our estuary environments are clean and protected from pollution and agricultural run-off.

MUSSELS

Another mollusc farmed in Australian waters is the mussel. Mussel farms are located in southern waters, in areas with good tidal flows, with the mussels growing on vertical ropes called longlines. In Australia, mussel farming started in Victoria in the 1970s and has since grown in popularity and spread to other southern states. Only one species of mussel is farmed in Australia: the Blue Mussel (*Mytilus galloprovincialis*). Mussel aquaculture is very sustainable, but some farms have problems with water quality and also attracting juvenile mussels, called spats, to the ropes. The mussels take 12–18 months to grow to market size.

People in Australia also consume clams, cockles, periwinkles, whelks, octopus and cuttlefish, which are mostly taken by recreational fishers, but also in a few minor commercial fisheries.

How are Pearls formed?

The most valuable part of any mollusc is not a shell or flesh, but an object that grows by accident within shelled molluscs – the pearl. Pearls have been used for jewellery for thousands of years and even today natural pearls command a high price.

Almost any shelled mollusc is capable of producing a natural pearl, but the best are produced by bivalve shells. The pearl is created when a parasite, sand or some other small intruder gets into the shell and the mollusc's immune system fights it. The mollusc does this by isolating the foreign object in a pearl sac, secreting calcium carbonate and a shiny substance called conchiolin to cover it. Over time the object is coated many times to create the pearls that people crave and desire. These natural pearls come in many shapes and colours, and round ones are very rare. The largest pearls are formed by giant clams, which have more of a porcelain finish and can weigh several kilograms.

South Sea Pearl Oysters are kept in racks at pearl farms as they grow.

Natural pearls are very rare, so most pearls produced today are cultured. This process involves implanting a graft (a piece of mantle tissue from another shell) and a round bead into the shell, which then forms a pearl sac. Cultural pearls are produced by both freshwater pearl mussels and marine pearl oysters.

Australia has a long tradition of pearling, which started with Aboriginals collecting pearl shells and either keeping them for their own uses or trading them with other tribes and also with Asian traders. After European settlement, pearl shells were collected in large numbers, first in Shark Bay, Western Australia, in the 1850s, followed by the Torres Strait, Queensland, in the 1860s, and finally Broome, Western Australia, in the 1880s. While natural pearls were found, most of these shells were collected to be turned into buttons. Fleets of pearl luggers worked these areas, deploying either free divers or divers using standard dress (hard hat divers) to collect the shells. Many of these divers were little more than slaves, with Japanese, Chinese and Aboriginals mainly doing the diving. The life expectancy of a pearl diver was very low, with drowning and getting

The goal of pearl farms is to produce perfectly formed pearls.

the bends among the hazards of the job. The mortality rate was very high, and many divers were forced to retire with crippling injuries.

The pearling industry based around the collection of pearl shells died off in the 1950s after the invention of plastic buttons, but this was also the time when the more lucrative pearl cultivation process started. Today pearl diving is a far safer activity, and Australia is one of the last countries to still use pearl divers to collect shells, which are then seeded to create cultured pearls. While pearl farming still occurs in a number of places in northern Australia, Broome is the centre of the pearl industry. The world's finest pearls come from Broome, cultured in the South Sea Pearl Oyster (*Pinctada maxima*). The pearl industry in Australia is today worth hundreds of millions of dollars.

MOLLUSC SPECIES

There are around 112,000 species of molluscs so far described, and many more species still waiting to be discovered. The molluscs are divided into seven classes based on their appearance and characteristics, however in this book we are only going to look at the four most common classes – the chitons, gastropods, bivalves and cephalopods. Within these classes are many species that divers, snorkelers and beachcombers will encounter in the seas around Australia.

CHITONS

Chitons

The chitons are a family of small marine molluscs that are easily overlooked, as they like to cling to rocks in very shallow water. The shell of a chiton is made up of eight overlapping plates, similar to a medieval knight's gauntlet, which has led to these creatures also being called coat-of-mail shells. These shells are actually part of the mantle and held together by a tough girdle. Although chitons are rarely seen moving, these overlapping plates give them great flexibility when crawling over rough surfaces.

Chitons are very basic molluscs, and many species look similar. However, these creatures vary in size (between 15mm and 300mm in length), have shell plates that differ greatly in shape and style, and some even have spines. Around 940 species of chitons are found in the oceans around the world, and while most species live in shallow water, a few have been found at great depths, up to 6,000m.

Chitons typically have a mantle that extends beyond the shell and have a large powerful foot. They mainly feed on algae, which they scrape off rocks with a rasp-like radula tongue, which is studded with rows of teeth. These teeth are unique in the animal world as they are coated with magnetite (a hard metal ferric/ferrous oxide mineral) and are the hardest teeth of any creature. Chitons are very slow moving, but with a powerful grip they are almost impossible to remove when clinging to a rock.

The Antique Chiton (*Callistochiton antiquus*) is found around Australia, but hidden under rocks is rarely seen.

The Giant Gem Chiton (*Acanthopleura gemmata*) is often found on rocks at low tide.

Some species live in such shallow water that they get exposed to the air at low tide, and can safely remain out of water for many hours at a time.

Chitons have sensory organs that are very different to those of other molluscs. The mantle and girdle have tactile nerve endings that allow the chiton to feel its surroundings. They also have a chemical sensing organ that allows them to find food. However, these strange little molluscs lack eyes, but they do possess small light sensing-organs across their shell that give them a very basic form of vision.

Chitons reproduce in several ways, depending on the species. The males release sperm into the water, which triggers the females to release their eggs. However, some female chitons draw the sperm into their mantle cavity to fertilise their eggs. The female then either lays eggs, which are attached to rocks, or retains the eggs internally until they are ready to hatch. Chitons are common around Australia, with 150 local species, although they are not always easy to find as many hide under rocks.

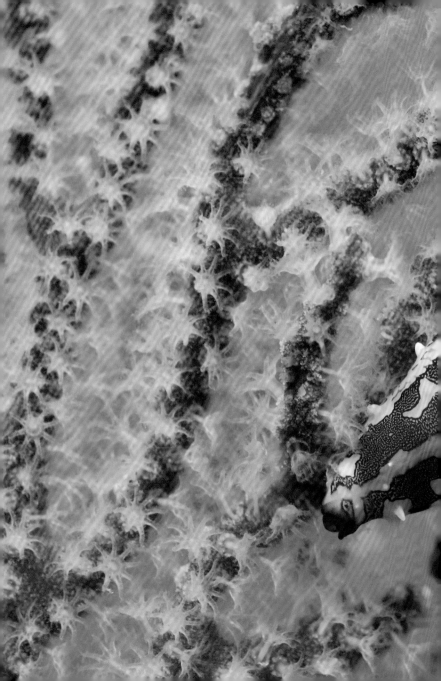

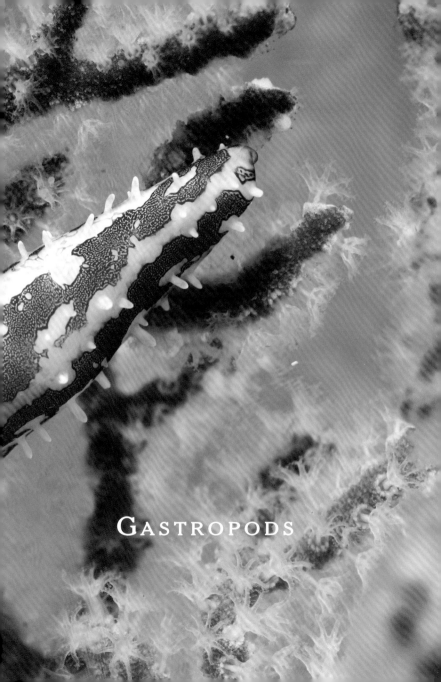

GASTROPODS

Gastropods

The largest family of molluscs. Once also known as univalves, and often simply referred to as snails and slugs, the gastropod family contains around 70,000 members. Members of this very diverse group of molluscs are found in habitats across the planet, and are not limited to saltwater, as many species live in freshwater and on land.

The gastropod family varies greatly and contains several subclasses or clades. The total number of subclasses, and how they fit together, has been revised and reviewed several times during the last decade, mainly based on new DNA analysis. This has caused much confusion, as new subclasses have been created, some have disappeared and others have been swapped around. But with such a large family this is to be expected and no doubt more changes will come in the future.

The main subclass is now the caenogastropods. This subclass contains around 100 families of molluscs with a hard coiled shell. The vetigastropod subclass contains 15 families that have a simple coiled or cone-shaped shell. The patellogastropod subclass contains the true limpets, while the very diverse heterobranch subclass contains mostly slug-like molluscs, such as the nudibranchs and sea hares, but also contains the land snails and slugs (which are not included in this book). There are two other subclasses within the gastropod family – neritopsina and cocculinid –

Nudibranchs are much loved by divers and are in the subclass heterobranch.

The beautiful cowries are a gastropod and in the subclass caenograstropod.

which are not often seen and therefore are not covered by this guide book.

As each subclass has different behavioural and biological features, they will be covered separately in order to look at typical families and species.

PATELLOGASTROPODS

The patellogastropod subclass contains the true limpets. There are a number of limpet-like shells also contained in other subclasses, but the true limpets are only found in saltwater. While most limpets live in the intertidal zone, a few species are found in the deep ocean, typically around hydrothermal vents.

LIMPETS

Limpets have a simple conical shell that covers the mantle. These creatures have a powerful foot, which is used to tenaciously cling to rocks to avoid being dislodged by waves and currents. Most features of the limpet are hidden under the shell. They have two tentacles on their head that are used to sense their environment, and two small eyes that can detect little more than light and shadows.

Limpets live about 10–20 years and breed by spawning. They generally spawn during the winter months, releasing eggs and sperm into the water column during storms. The young larvae drift for weeks, before settling on the rocky bottom and metamorphosing into their adult form.

The Weaver Limpet is the most common limpet species in Australia and found in rock pools.

Limpets feed on algae, which they scrape off rocks with tough teeth on their radula. They are slow-moving and rarely stray more than one metre from a favourite attachment point. These small molluscs have an incredibly strong grip and are almost impossible to remove without a knife. They achieve this grip with suction from their muscular foot and with the aid of an adhesive mucus.

Limpets can be observed on most rocky surfaces in shallow water, even in rock pools. They often get exposed at low tide and can survive a dry spell by trapping water under their shell. Limpets are a vital species in the intertidal zone, as they keep the algae in check so that other creatures can share this habitat. Many limpet species are found around Australia, and most of these small shells are less than 3cm in diameter. One of the most common species is the Weaver Limpet (*Cellana tramoserica*), which can grow to a width of 6cm.

VETIGASTROPODS

Only found in marine environments, this is considered to be a primitive group of gastropods. The subclass contains 15 families, including the pheasant snails, keynote limpets, turbans, slit shells and top shells, with the abalone the best-known member of the group. Found in a range of marine habitats from shallow to deep water, vetigastropods typically have an oval-shaped shell, which can be either spiralled or conical, and many species have secondary shell openings. A common feature of this group is also an intersected cross-plated shell structure.

Vetigastropods utilise a variety of different food sources, depending on the family and species. Many are grazers, feeding on algae, while others feed on sponges, bryozoans and ascidians. The reproduction strategy of this group also varies between species, as a few deep-water species are hermaphrodites, but most species have separate sexes. Some lay jelly-like eggs on the bottom, while others release eggs and sperm directly into the water.

The body structure of vetigastropods is similar to that of patellogastropods, with the shell covering the mantle, a powerful foot and a functional head with sensory tentacles, eyes and a mouth. Most shells in this family have dull colouration on the exterior.

ABALONES

The most highly prized members of the vetigastropod family. Abalones have an open oval-shaped spiral shell, which on the inner side has a polished mirror-like lustre. Known as mother-of-pearl, this material has been used for jewellery and other decorative objects for thousands of years. However, the real value of the abalone is its flesh, which is considered a delicacy and commands a high price.

The Blacklip Abalone only moves about at night.

The abalone family contains more than 50 species found around the world. Most species live in shallow water, in depths to 30m, and vary in size from 2–30cm in diameter. Also known as ear shells, because of the shape of their shell, abalone shells have a series of holes in the outer surface that are respiratory pores.

Most abalone species live in cooler temperate waters and feed on algae at night. During the day they

The Circular Abalone is a smaller species mainly seen at night.

The most highly prized abalone in Australian is the Greenlip Abalone.

generally shelter in caves and on ledges, gripping the rock surface with their powerful foot. Smaller species hide under rocks and are not often seen.

Being in such high demand, bag limits are set on how many abalone you can take in Australia, and commercial operations are licensed. About a quarter of all abalone consumed comes from Tasmania. The two most commonly collected species in Australia are the Greenlip Abalone (*Haliotis laevigata*) and the Blacklip Abalone (*Haliotis rubra*). Both species reach a size of around 20cm, with the Greenlip Abalone the most highly prized of the two. Two other species are also collected in lesser numbers: Brownlip Abalone (*Haliotis conicopora*) and Roe's Abalone (*Haliotis roei*). Australia is also home to a number of smaller abalone species, such as the Circular Abalone (*Haliotis cyclobates*), which is common in southern waters and is rarely more than 10cm wide.

PHEASANT SNAILS

Another family in this subclass that are seen by divers are the pheasant snails. These small molluscs have a round-shaped shell with a short spiral. Pheasant shells feed on algae, and are generally found in shallow water. Around 130 species are known in temperate and tropical waters. A common species seen in Australia's southern waters is the Ventricose Pheasant Shell (*Phasianella ventricosa*). This pretty small shell has a smooth finish and very detailed patterns across its surface. Growing to 5cm in length, this species is quite common in South Australia and is found on rocky reefs with a good covering of kelp and seaweed.

The Ventricose Pheasant Shell is often seen in South Australia.

CAENOGASTROPODS

Most sea shells found washed up on the beach are members of the large caenogastropod family. Almost all members of this subclass possess a hard external shell. This shell, which can vary greatly in shape and style, is generally coiled into a tube. However, some species only have a coiled shell in the larval stage, which becomes a conical structure as the animal grows. Most species live in marine habitats, in both shallow and deep water, but some members of this subclass live in freshwater, and a few species also live on land.

Caenogastropods typically have a large foot for mobility, a head, and a mantle protected by the shell. The head is well formed in some species, and basic in others, and features two eyes on the ends of tentacles and a retractable proboscis with radula for feeding. All the vital organs are contained within the mantle.

In this class of molluscs the male has a penis located in its neck. The female similarly has a sexual organ in the neck, and most species mate neck-to-neck using internal fertilisation. However, a number of species also use external fertilisation. The great majority of marine caenogastropods have separate sexes, but most land species are hermaphrodites, having both male and female sex organs.

There are more than 100 families of sea shells within the caenogastropod subclass, and if we were to include every one, this book would turn into an encyclopedia. Instead this guide will look at some of the common families and species that are easy to view underwater or washed up on beaches around Australia.

AUGERS

Named after auger drills, because of their elongated screw-like shape, augers are very pretty shells that generally live on sandy bottoms. Around 300 species of augers are known, and most members of this family reside in warm tropical seas. Rarely seen during the day, augers dig into the sand and emerge at night to feed. They typically feed on worms and stun their prey with a venomous barb. Most augers are 4–15cm long, but a few species grow to more than 20cm in length.

Augers, like this Dimidiate Auger (top), are typically found in the sand, but at night they will move across rocks and coral looking for prey, like this Flowery Auger (bottom).

Numerous species of augers are found in Australia's tropical waters, but they are best observed at night. The shape of their shells varies greatly – some are very long and thin, while others are quite short. Two very attractive species found in Australia are the Flowery Auger (*Terebra chlorata*) and the Dimidiate Auger (*Terebra dimidiata*).

CONES

A pretty family and one that is best avoided as many cones are highly venomous. Containing more than 800 species, cones come in a wide variety of shapes and colours. Many members of this family have beautifully patterned shells, but others are quite plain. Identifying species can sometimes be difficult, as many individuals get a covering of algae on the shell.

Like many mollusc species, cones are more active by night when they emerge from daytime hiding spots to stalk prey. Cones are very skilled hunters and like to consume fish, worms and other molluscs. They stun their prey with poisonous darts shot out of a proboscis, which are actually modified radula, and

A variety of cones can be found in Australia's tropical waters, such as the Striated Cone (top), Marble Cone (middle), Geographic Cone (bottom left) and the Textile Cone (bottom right).

then the prey is swallowed whole. This poison varies in strength between species, but with at least 30 human fatalities from cones, all should be treated with respect and not touched or handled.

Cones are found throughout the Indo-Pacific region, and while they are more common in tropical waters, there are also a few found in Australia's temperate seas. One of the most colourful members of this family is the Textile Cone (*Conus textile*), which occurs in tropical waters and also in northern New South Wales. Two other pretty species that share the same range are the Geography Cone (*Conus geographus*) and the Striated Cone (*Conus striatus*). The Marble Cone (*Conus marmoreus*) is another striking member of the family found in tropical waters.

COWRIES

Without doubt the most beautiful of all the sea shells are the cowries. Coveted by humans for thousands of years, for decoration and even currency, cowries dazzle with their wonderful colours and sheen. These lovely shells extend a mantle that covers the shell, keeping it clean and shiny throughout the animal's life. Around 200 species of cowries have been discovered. Most cowries are tropical, but numerous temperate species are known, and the ones from southern Australia are very highly prized by shell collectors.

Cowries are typically oval shaped, but many species that live on corals, and are commonly known as allied cowries, are elongated. Cowries feed on a wide variety of foods, including sponges, algae, soft corals and other molluscs, while some even scavenge on dead animals.

A lovely Snake's Head Cowry from Western Australia.

Cowries come in wide variety of shapes and colour patterns; including the Honey Cowry (top left), Spotted Cowry (top right), Sieve Cowry (middle left), Milk-spot Cowry (middle right), Black Cowry (bottom left) and Tiger Cowry (bottom right).

Egg cowries are typical found on their food source, corals. Australian species include Draper's Egg Cowry (top left), Egg Cowry (top right), Beautiful Egg Cowry (bottom left) and Toenail Egg Cowry (bottom right).

A common species found throughout the tropical Indo-Pacific region is the Tiger Cowry (*Cypraea tigris*); this large shell can grow to 10cm in length. A similar-looking species from southern Australia is the Black Cowry (*Zoila thersites*); this species can also reach a length of 10cm and is mostly seen at night when it emerges to feed.

In tropical waters a wonderful variety of small cowries can be seen, including Honey Cowry (*Cypraea helvolva*), Milk-spot Cowry (*Cypraea vitellus*), Spotted Cowry (*Cypraea punctata*), Snake's Head Cowry (*Cypraea caputserpentis kenyonae*) and Sieve Cowry (*Cypraea cribaria*). Some of the prettiest cowries are also known as egg cowries, as they are usually a white colour. Often found sitting on its favourite food of soft coral is the striking Egg Cowry (*Ovula ovum*). With its white shell and black mantle this is a species that is hard to miss. A harder species to find is the Toe-nail Egg Cowry (*Calpurnus verrucosus*), as it is much smaller and often hidden in the folds of the soft coral. Even smaller allied egg cowries are found on fan corals, such as the Beautiful Egg Cowry (*Crenavolva aureola*) and Draper's Egg Cowry (*Cuspivolva draperi*).

The most spectacular of all the cowries are the allied cowries, especially a group known as spindle cowries. These are often difficult to find as their mantles often

Spindle cowries are elongated and beautiful shells, lookout for the Rosy Spindle Cowry (top left), Graceful Spingle Cowry (above) and Angus Spindle Cowry (bottom left).

match the colouration and texture of their host coral. Wonderful tropical species include the Rosy Spindle Cowry (*Phenacovolva rosea*), Graceful Spindle Cowry (*Phenacovolva gracilis*) and Angus's Spindle Cowry (*Phenacovolva angasi*).

CREEPERS

Often confused with the augers, the creepers are small elongated horn-shaped shells that are generally covered in intricate patterns. Most species are less than 5cm long, but larger members of the family can grow to 15cm in length. Creepers live in shallow water and graze on algae, and can be found on rocky reefs, coral reefs and sandy bottoms. Around 120 species of creepers have been described, and divers mostly see these lovely little shells at night.

A common species of creeper seen in tropical waters is the Rough Creeper (*Rhinoclavis aspera*). This species is often seen in sandy lagoons on the Great Barrier Reef. A species more commonly seen around coral rubble is the Nodulose Creeper (*Cerithium nodulosum*) – this species has a very decorative shell and can reach a length of 15cm.

The Nodulose Creeper is found on the Great Barrier Reef.

DOG WHELKS

Also known as mud snails, members of this family of small molluscs are typically found in shallow water. These predatory snails feed on other molluscs by drilling into the shell and sucking out their body juices. They are also scavengers, and perform an important task of consuming dead marine animals. Around 300 species of dog whelks have been described, and they typically have a short spiral shell. Dog whelks are mostly found on sandy and muddy bottoms, but some are also found in rock pools. They are more commonly seen at night, however they will emerge during the day if a dead fish is nearby.

The two most common dog whelks seen around Australia are the Pimpled Dog Whelk (above left) and the Reticulated Dog Whelk (above right).

A number of dog whelk species are found in both tropical and temperate waters around Australia. A widespread species is the Reticulated Dog Whelk (*Nassarius particeps*), which grows to 3cm in length and is found almost everywhere around the country. A common tropical species is the Pimpled Dog Whelk (*Nassarius papillosus*); it grows to a length of 5cm and has nodules all over its shell.

HELMETS

The helmet shells are all medium-sized to large shells that are shaped like a soldier's helmet. This family contains around 80 members that typically have a solid shell with a short coiled spire and flared rim shield at the base. Many species also have prominent horns and nodules on the coiled part of the shell. Helmet shells are found in both tropical and warm temperate waters, and are generally found on sandy bottoms, as most species hide under the sand by day.

Helmet shells feed on seastars and sea urchins, and they use their heavy shells to crush sea urchin shells and spines. The urchins naturally fight back and even impale the helmets with their poisonous spines, but the snail releases an enzyme that

Helmet shells vary greatly in size, from the small Banded Helmet (above left) to the large Giant Helmet (top right).

protects it from the urchin's toxins. The helmet breaks down the sea urchin's hard shell by secreting sulphuric acid, and then consumes the dissolved remains.

The most common member of this family seen by divers and snorkelers in tropical Australia is the Giant Helmet (*Cassis cornuta*). Also known as the Horned Helmet, this is the largest member of the family and can grow to 40cm in length. It is often seen on sandy or rubble bottoms, and because of its large size it doesn't often bury itself so can be observed by day. Most other helmet species are much smaller and remain hidden under a layer of sand during the day, so are only observed at night. One species that divers can see in tropical waters by night is the Banded Helmet (*Phalium bandatum*) – this pretty shell grows to 14cm in length and feeds on sand dollar urchins.

MOON SNAILS

Moon snails have a shell that is very similar in shape to the shell of common garden snails. This family contains around 270 species that are found in both shallow and

deep water in tropical and temperate seas. Moon snails are highly efficient predators that feed on other shelled molluscs and sometimes also on crabs. When a moon snail finds another shell it will engulf its prey with its large foot and then proceed to bore through the shell with the radula. They also secrete acid

The Oriental Moon Snail emerges from the sand at night to feed.

to soften the shell. Once they bore through the shell they consume the flesh of the mollusc with their proboscis.

Most moon snails are typically small, only 2–6cm long, and being nocturnal they spend the day hidden under a layer of sand. The most common moon snail that divers encounter at night in the tropical waters of Australia is the Oriental Moon Snail (*Naticarius orientalis*); this species grows to 6cm in length and has a yellow shell and a pretty orange-and-white patterned foot.

MUREXES

One of the most diverse and fascinating families of shells. More than 1,500 species have been described, and they vary greatly in size and appearance. Some murex species have very fancy shells, decorated with spines, horns, ruffles and very long tails, while others are quite plain, with the shell only decorated with a covering of nodules. Many of the plainer species are simply called rock shells.

Most murexes are carnivores, preying on other molluscs and barnacles. They often bore through the shell of their prey with their radula, then devour the soft flesh. Murexes are found around the world in both deep and shallow water, and they are most commonly found on sandy bottoms.

The most spectacular members of this family have long tails and are covered in spines, like the Spiny Murex (*Murex acanthostephes*); this species is found in Australia's tropical north, but is rarely seen. A more common tropical species is the Giant Murex (*Chicoreus ramosus*), which is covered in blunt horns and reaches a length of 30cm. The closely related Rose-branch Murex (*Chicoreus palmarosae*) is covered in branching horns and reaches a length of 15cm.

A plain murex species commonly encountered on coral reefs is the Dogwood Drupe (*Drupella conus*) – a small murex that feeds on hard corals and can

The most beautiful members of the murex family have delicate spikes, like this Spiny Murex.

sometimes be found in large numbers. Another plain species commonly seen in shallow water is the Mulberry Shell (*Morula marginalba*). This distinctive black-and-white shell only grows to 3cm in length and is common throughout the northern half of Australia. Feeding on barnacles and worms, Mulberry Shells are often found clinging to rocks in the intertidal zone.

On this page is a collection of murex shells that shows how greatly they vary in design: Dogwood Drupe (top left), Rose-branch Murex (top right), Mulberry Shells (middle) and a Giant Murex (bottom).

SPINDLES

Typically reddish-brown and named for their spindle-like shape. Some members of this family can grow quite large, to more than 50cm long, however their typical size is generally 10–20cm in length. Spindles are found in both tropical and temperate seas, with around 200 species so far discovered. These carnivores, which feed on other molluscs, worms and barnacles, are found in shallow and deep water, and appear to be just as common on reefs as they are on sandy bottoms.

While a number of spindle species can be seen around Australia, one of the most common is the Southern Spindle (*Fasciolaria australasia*), which can be seen almost anywhere but is far more abundant in cooler southern waters. Southern Spindles grow to a length of 18cm, and are often seen resting on the bottom during the day.

The Southern Spindle is common in southern waters.

STROMBS

One of the most beautiful and distinctive shell families. They are similar to other members of this suborder in having a spiral shell, however with a fanned outer edge most species appear quite flattened. Two features also set strombs apart from other shell species. They have two well-developed eyes, which sit on the end of stalk-like tentacles to give the animal a great range of vision. They also have a unique way of moving about, as attached to the end of the foot is a curved blade-like nail called

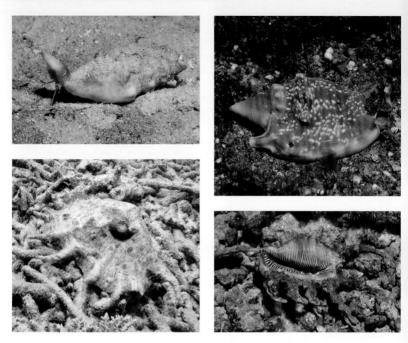

Strombs are typical found on sand or rubble and common species include the Vomer Stromb (top left), Bubble Stromb (top right), Seba's Spider Shell (bottom left) and the Scorpion Spider Shell (bottom right).

an operculum. In order to move the animal digs the tip of this operculum into the substrate and pulls itself forward.

Strombs are most commonly found in the Indo-Pacific region, and around 150 species have been described. Most are found in shallow water, and feeding on macroalgae they live on sandy or muddy bottoms. The best-known members of the family are the spider shells. Several of these attractive shells are found in Australia's tropical waters, including the very common Seba's Spider Shell (*Lambis truncata sebae*) and the less common Scorpion Spider Shell (*Lambis scorpius*). The top surface of these shells is generally quite plain or can be covered in algae, while the underside is shiny and brilliantly coloured. Spider shells are large members of the stromb family, and can grow up to 30cm long.

Most other stromb species are much smaller, less than 10cm long, such as the Bubble Stromb (*Strombus bulla*) and the Vomer Stromb (*Strombus vomer*). These tropical species live on sandy bottoms and lie hidden in the sand by day, emerging at night to feed.

TRITONS

Common in both tropical and temperate seas, with around 150 members in the family. Tritons vary greatly in size, but all have a similar spiral shape and a large opening for the foot to emerge. Also known as trumpet shells, in ancient times the ends were cut off so that the shell could be blown like a trumpet. However, tritons are actually named after the Greek god Triton, who is often depicted holding one of these shells.

The Giant Triton (top left) is the largest member of this family. Spengler's Triton (top right) shells are often used by hermit crabs. The small Banded Tadpole Triton (bottom left) has hairs on its shell. A Giant Triton (bottom right) searching for seastars.

Tritons are carnivores, and feed on other molluscs and also seastars. Like most molluscs they are nocturnal and spend the day hidden among corals or rocks, or under a layer of sand. When they detect a seastar they give chase. Some seastars are thought to be able to sense the nearby presence of a triton and flee. However, the tritons are generally faster and grab their prey with their muscular foot. They then cut through the tough skin of the seastar with their radula teeth, releasing a poisonous saliva to paralyse the prey. The seastar is then slowly consumed.

Many triton species are found around Australia. The Giant Triton (*Charonia tritonis*) is a very important species. It is the largest member of the family and grows to 50cm in length. Found throughout Australia's tropical waters, it is particularly important to the health of the hard corals of the Great Barrier Reef as it feeds on Crown-of-thorns

Seastars (*Acanthaster planci*). Unfortunately, at present the species is not found in large numbers, but a breeding program is underway in order to increase its numbers and hopefully keep Crown-of-thorns numbers in check.

Most other triton species are much smaller, only 2–10cm long. A smaller species also seen in tropical waters is the Banded Tadpole Triton (*Gyrineum gyrinum*), which only grows to 3cm in length and is unusual as the shell is covered in short hairy filaments. A common species in temperate waters is Spengler's Triton (*Cabestana spengleri*), which favours rocky reefs and is a popular shell for hermit crabs to use as a mobile home.

VIOLET SNAILS

Often found washed up on beaches around Australia, violet snails are small round-shelled molluscs that live on the surface of the ocean. These creatures float on the surface with the aid of a mucus bubble float and feed on Bluebottles (*Physalia utriculus*). Around ten species of violet snails are known, and being at the complete mercy of wind and currents, they often get washed up on beaches. Most violet snails have a purple shell, including the Purple Violet Snail (*Janthina janthina*), which is common right around Australia and has a more squat shell than other species.

The Purple Violet Snail often washes up on Australian beaches.

WENTLETRAPS

This family of small spiral-shaped shells is closely related to the violet snails. Named after the Dutch word for spiral staircase, these small shells are also known as staircase shells and ladder shells. The wentletrap family contains around 630 members, and most species feed on corals and anemones. While most wentletrap shells are white, the most common species that divers encounter in Australia is the pretty

The Golden Wentletrap feeds on tubastrea corals.

Golden Wentletrap (*Epidendrium billeeanum*). This species grows to a length of 2cm and is commonly found feeding on tubastrea corals in tropical and subtropical waters.

This Baler Shell (top left) is in the process of laying eggs. Volutes are most active at night, emerging from the sand to feed; common species around Australia include the Lightning Volute (top right), Beautiful Volute (bottom left) and Mitre-like Volute (bottom right).

VOLUTES

Named after the Latin word for scroll, this is an exceptionally attractive family of molluscs and its members vary greatly in size. Shells in this family typically have an elongated spiral shape with wonderful decorative patterns. Around 250 species of volutes have been described, and they are usually found on sandy bottoms, as most species feed and hide in this habitat. Volutes are carnivores and feed on a range of other species, including fish, echinoderms and other molluscs.

Volutes have always been collected by people for display and decoration. Australian Aboriginals gathered larger species to eat and also used these shells to carry and store water. Volutes are more commonly found in tropical seas, however many temperate species are found in southern Australia. The largest volute species, the spectacular Baler Shell (*Melo amphora*), is found in Australia's tropical seas. This huge shell can reach a length of 50cm, although specimens measuring more than 30cm long are rare. Most other volute species are much smaller, varying in size from 5–15cm long. Another wonderful tropical species is the Beautiful Volute (*Cymbiola pulchra*) – like most members of its family this species is mostly seen at night when it emerges to feed.

In southern temperate waters one of the most common species is the Lightning Volute (*Ericusa fulgetra*); this species is observed by divers at night, moving quickly across the sandy seafloor on its large foot with its proboscis waving about in search of food. Another nocturnal species seen in the same range is the pretty Mitre-like Volute (*Lyria mitraeformis*), which only grows to 5cm in length and has ridges and patterns on its shell that are very different to those of other volute species.

HETEROBRANCHS

Heterobranchs

One of the largest and most diverse groups of gastropods can be found in the heterobranch subclass. Recently revised, this group contains many molluscs that lack a shell, have a greatly reduced shell, or have an internal shell. Many species within this family could be called sea slugs, and while numerous species are found in saltwater, this large subclass also incorporates many land molluscs, including the snails and slugs.

To simplify things, the heterobranch subclass is split into three subdivisions based on their common features: lower heterobranch, opisthobranch and pulmonata. The lower heterobranch subdivision includes families of marine and freshwater shells, and is not included in this book. The opisthobranch subdivision contains some of the most interesting and colourful families of molluscs that are all sea slug shaped, including the bubble shells, sea hares, sapsuckers, side-gilled slugs and nudibranchs.

The pulmonata subdivision contains all the land snail and slug families, and also a few freshwater varieties, which are not included in this guide.

As there are many family differences within the opisthobranch subdivision, this guide will look at the families in this group individually, and also some of the typical species that can be encountered around Australia.

Sea hares form into mating chains when they breed.

BUBBLE SHELLS

The name of this order of molluscs is a little misleading, as not all bubble shells have external shells. Also known as headshield slugs, because of their typically broad head, these sea slugs generally have a small bubble-like shell that is often too small for the animal to retract into when threatened. However, many bubble shells lack a shell or have an internal shell, so other features are generally used to identify members of this order.

Lined Bubble Shell.

The wide headshield is a common feature. This broad head is generally used to plough through or into sand, as many bubble shells hide under a layer of sand during the day. The headshield also contains small eyes and numerous sensory cilia around the mouth, which are used to detect and track prey. Many bubble shells look similar to the closely related nudibranchs, but they lack rhinophores (sensory tentacles on the head) and external gills, which are typical characteristics of a nudibranch. Many bubble shells also have fleshy wings, known as parapodia, which enclose the shell or curl up over the body. In some species these parapodia are actually used as wings, allowing the animal to flap them and swim away from danger.

Bubble shells consume a wide variety of food, depending on the species. Some eat algae, others sponges, and many are predators that feed on worms, nudibranchs and even other bubble

Rose Petal Bubble Shell.

shells. Predatory bubble shells swallow their prey whole and then crush them between gizzard plates. Like most members of the heterobranch group they are hermaphrodites, possessing both male and female sexual organs, which are located in the neck. During mating they fertilise their partner's eggs, which are then deposited on the bottom in jelly-like strings.

Around 600 species of bubble shell have been described, and Australia is home to numerous species of these pretty molluscs. The most common member of this

family seen in Australia is the Rose
Petal Bubble Shell (*Hydatina physis*),
which is common off New South Wales,
Queensland and Western Australia;
this large bubble shell grows to 5cm in
length and is generally found on sandy
bottoms. Another common species is the
Lined Bubble Shell (*Bullina lineata*); this
species occurs in a similar range, and
has an attractive shell with fine red lines,
while its body is white and transparent.
It reaches a length of 2cm and feeds on
worms.

Taronga Headshield Slug.

Another common species that shares
a similar range is the Variable Headshield
Slug (*Chelidonura varians*). This species
has no visible shell, and is black in
colour with a bright blue trim. This slug
lives in the sand and emerges to feed
on flatworms. A species that divers will
see in southern waters is the Taronga
Headshield Slug (*Philinopsis taronga*).
This species also lacks a visible shell and
is typically a brownish colour with white
spots. Growing to a length of 4cm, this
slug feeds on other molluscs.

Variable Headshield Slug.

SEA HARES

Generally found in shallow water, and
even washed up on beaches, the sea
hares are marine sea slugs that feed on
algae and seaweed. Named for their
large oral tentacles, which look similar
to rabbit or hare ears, sea hares typically
have an elongated body and fleshy
parapodia wings on their backs that are
used for swimming. Sea hares appear
to be shell-less sea slugs, however they
do have a small shell contained within
the body mantle that protects their vital
organs.

Extraordinary Sea Hare.

The Geographic Sea Hare is only seen at night.

Eared Sea Hare.

Black-tailed Sea Hare.

Sea hares have small rhinophores on their head and tiny eyes that see little more than light and shadows. These sea slugs vary greatly in size, from small species only a few centimetres long to giants measuring more than 50cm in length. To avoid predators, sea hares can swim, but they can also create a getaway 'smokescreen' by squirting purple ink from special ink glands. Similar to other heterobranch members they are hermaphrodites, and after mating they lay eggs in spaghetti-like clumps. When mating, sea hares sometimes form into a long queue or mating chain, and die soon after laying their eggs, after a short one year lifespan.

Sea hares are common in both tropical and temperate waters, with many species seen around Australia. One of the most widespread and common species is the Black-tailed Sea Hare (*Aplysia argus*). This species is found in tropical and warm temperate seas and can grow to a length of 30cm.

Another widespread species is the Extraordinary Sea Hare (*Aplysia extraordinaria*). This giant member of the family can grow to 40cm in length and is found off the east coast of Australia. It comes in a range of colours – many are just a plain green or brown, but some have a pretty red or orange colouration. A more unusual sea hare species to look out for is the Eared Sea Hare (*Dolabella auricularia*), which is another widespread tropical species that grows to 30cm in length. It has warty or furry skin, which makes it well camouflaged when feeding on algae, and also comes in a range of colours – it is possible that the colour of an individual may vary depending upon the type of algae it is consuming. A species generally only seen at night is the pretty Geographic Sea Hare (*Syphonota geographica*), which appears to bury itself in the sand during the day, emerging to feed at sunset. This species is found throughout the Indo-West Pacific, but is not often seen due to its nocturnal habits.

SAPSUCKERS

Sapsuckers are small sea slugs that many people easily overlook or confuse with their better-known cousins, the nudibranchs. Sapsuckers differ from nudibranchs in having no external gills, and most species have prominent parapodia flaps that run along the back for the entire length of the body. Other species have elaborate fleshy flaps that cover their upper body and are known as cerata. These tiny sea slugs have small rhinophores and very small eyes. Most sapsucker species lack a shell, but several families have small shells, which can lead to confusion with the bubble shells. Similar to other members of the heterobranch group, sapsuckers are hermaphrodites, mating at the neck and laying ribbon-like eggs on the seafloor.

Sapsuckers have a single row of teeth or radula, and most species feed on algae, sucking the cells or sap out, hence their unusual name. However, some species also feed on fish eggs or the eggs of other molluscs. These tiny sea slugs are rarely more

Green Sapsucker.

Ocellate Sapsucker.

Ornate Sapsucker.

Splendid Sapsucker.

than 3cm long. They are also well camouflaged, taking on the colouration of the algae they consume. Around 280 species of sapsucker have been identified. These creatures are commonly found throughout the tropical waters of the Indo-Pacific region, but are less common in Australia's temperate waters.

Most sapsuckers are typically green in colour, like the widespread Ornate Sapsucker (*Elysia ornata*), which is common throughout the Indo-West Pacific region. Other species are multi-coloured, such as the pretty Splendid Sapsucker (*Thuridilla splendens*) that is also found throughout the Indo-West Pacific region. While most sapsucker species are found on algae, the Ocellate Sapsucker (*Plakobranchus ocellatus*) is more commonly seen on sandy bottoms throughout the Indo-West Pacific region. The shells on most sapsuckers are barely noticeable, but one exception is the Green Sapsucker (*Oxynoe viridis*), which has a bubble-like shell on its back and is a vivid green colour with blue spots; this is another species common throughout the Indo-West Pacific region, and found off New South Wales and Queensland.

SOLAR-POWERED SEA SLUGS

Many sapsuckers feed on algae, digesting the algae cells for nutrients. Usually the consumption process ends there, but some of these unusual creatures use the digested algae cells in a very bizarre way and could be called 'solar-powered sea slugs'. These sapsuckers (and also a few nudibranch species) retain and utilise the living chloroplasts (special subunits in plant cells that carry out photosynthesis) within their own tissues. This recycling process is known as kleptoplasty, and is generally only found in single-celled creatures. Sapsuckers that use this process are believed to obtain extra nutrients from these chloroplasts that continue to photosynthesise within the slug.

SIDE-GILLED SLUGS

The side-gilled slugs are another mollusc family that has recently been restructured and split into two groups. The side-gilled slugs typically have plume-like gills on the right side of their body, between the foot and mantle. These sea slugs are often quite large, with many more than 10cm long, and have a broad foot, two cylindrical rhinophores and two oral tentacles.

Forskal's Slug.

The recent restructuring of this family has seen the side-gilled slugs classified as either umbraculida or pleurobranchomorpha. Members of the umbraculida have a small mantle and a visible external shell, which is usually flat and limpet-like, while pleurobranchomorpha members have either a small internal shell or no shell at all, plus a large mantle. Members of this group are often mistaken for nudibranchs, but lack external gills.

Side-gilled slugs are carnivores, feeding on sponges, ascidians, anemones, other molluscs and even other side-gilled slugs, which are consumed using strong jaws and broad radula. Many species of side-gilled slugs use chemical weapons for defence, secreting toxins from a mantle gland. These toxins vary between

Moon-faced Slug.

species, with some producing sulphuric acid and others secreting poisons that are similar to blue-ringed octopus venom. Like other heterobranch families, side-gilled slugs are hermaphrodites.

Many species of side-gilled slugs are found around Australia, and these creatures are mainly seen at night when they emerge to feed. Two members of the umbraculida group that divers encounter are the Umbrella Shell (*Umbraculum umbraculum*) and Small Umbrella Shell (*Tylodina corticalis*). Both species are found in New South Wales and Queensland, however the Small Umbrella Shell also occurs off Victoria, South Australia and Western Australia. Both species feed on sponges.

Members of the pleurobranchomorpha family are more commonly seen by divers

Small Umbrella Shell.

Umbrella Shell.

at night. They are generally found on sandy bottoms, with species such as the Moon-faced Slug (*Euselenops luniceps*) and Forskal's Slug (*Pleurobranchus forskalii*) found throughout the Indo-West Pacific, and off Queensland and New South Wales.

NUDIBRANCHS

The best-known members of the heterobranch family, especially among divers who seek out these remarkable critters, are the nudibranchs. Often called the butterflies of the sea, because they come in such an extraordinary range of colour combinations, nudibranchs are soft-bodied sea slugs that lack a shell.

Nudibranchs are found around the planet in all marine environments. They are most commonly seen in tropical seas, but also occur in temperate seas, deep water and even Antarctica. Nudibranchs eat a wide variety of food, depending on the species. Sponges are commonly taken, but these colourful sea slugs also eat ascidians, hydroids, algae, anemones, corals and even other nudibranchs. Their radula teeth vary depending on what they eat, and are used by researchers to identify different species. Recently researchers have used DNA samples to identify and classify species, which has led to a major shake-up in the nudibranch family.

These wonderful creatures typically have gills on their back (the name nudibranch in Latin means naked gills), a set of rhinophores, oral tentacles and a mantle that extends over the foot. However, with more than 2,300 species of nudibranchs, and many families within the order, these sea slugs come in a wide variety of shapes and sizes. Some nudibranchs have no visible gills, others have a hard body, and some are covered in fleshy growths known as cerata. As such the nudibranch order is split into four suborders based on these differences.

HARLEQUIN NUDIBRANCHS

The harlequin nudibranchs (or doridaceans) are the most common species that divers encounter around Australia, and typically have a plain body with feathery gills on their back. Other families within this suborder have nodules over their bodies, and others have no visible gills. One of the largest and most common species found in the southern waters of Australia is the Short-tailed Ceratosoma (*Ceratosoma brevicaudatum*), which can grow to 10cm in length and varies in colour from yellow to orange. The closely related Yellow-ridged Ceratosoma (*Ceratosoma flavicostatum*) is a tropical species found off Queensland and New South Wales.

Co's Goniobranchus (*Goniobranchus coi*) is often seen on the Great Barrier Reef. Another pretty tropical species that is also found in New South Wales is the Purple-spotted Goniobranchus (*Goniobranchus aureopurpurea*), while a spectacular species divers see in Queensland and northern New South Wales is the Red-girdled

Co's Goniobranchus.

Denison's Dendrodoris.

Gold-spotted Halgerda.

Ocellate Phyllidia.

Purple-spotted Goniobranchus.

Red-girdled Ardeadoris.

Short-tailed Ceratosoma.

Verco's Verconia.

Verco's Tambja.

Yellow-ridged Ceratosoma.

Ardeadoris (*Ardeadoris rubroannulata*). One of the most striking species found in southern Australia is Verco's Tambja (*Tambja verconis*), and another lovely species that divers see in southern waters is the Verco's Verconia (*Verconia verconis*).

Black-rayed Fryeria.

Other families with the harlequin nudibranch suborder have nodules on their bodies. Denison's Dendrodoris (*Dendrodoris denisoni*) and the Gold-spotted Halgerda (*Halgerda aurantiomaculata*) both have prominent nodules and are found in Queensland and New South Wales. Many species within the harlequin nudibranch suborder also have firm bodies and no visible gills, such as the Ocellate Phyllidia (*Phyllidia ocellata*) and the Black-rayed Fryeria (*Fryeria picta*); both these species are found in tropical waters and have the gills hidden under the mantle.

TUBERCULAR NUDIBRANCHS

The tubercular nudibranchs (or aeolidaceans) are covered in rows of finger-like growths called cerata. The tips of these cerata contain stinging cells obtained from eating hydroids (see Nudibranch Secret Weapons). A very common member of this suborder is the Blue Dragon Pteraeolidia (*Pteraeolidia ianthina*), a wonderful nudibranch that is often found in Queensland and New South Wales. A more widespread tropical species is the Much-desired Flabellina (*Flabellina exoptata*), a beautiful nudibranch frequently seen feasting on hydroids in Western Australia, Queensland and New South Wales. Another colourful member of this suborder is the Indian Phidiana (*Phidiana indica*), which occurs throughout the Indo-West Pacific and has a striking orange or red head. The Great Phyllodesmium (*Phyllodesmium magnum*) has very elaborate cerata, grows to 10cm in length and is found in tropical and subtropical waters right around Australia.

Indian Phidiana (above) and Blue Dragon Pteraeolidia (below).

Great Phyllodesmium.

Much-desired Flabellina.

Elegant Tritoniopsis (above) and Snakey Bornella (below).

BACK-GILLED NUDIBRANCHS

The back-gilled nudibranchs (or dentrotaceans) generally have two rows of branching gills along their back. Members of this suborder are less common, and many species are well camouflaged and therefore difficult to find. One of the more frequently encountered species is the Elegant Tritoniopsis (*Tritoniopsis elegans*), which is generally white, although yellow, orange and even pink specimens have been recorded; divers will find this species in New South Wales and Queensland. The Snakey Bornella (*Bornella anguilla*) is a tropical species and is one of the few nudibranchs that can swim. This is probably how the species got its name, as when it swims in moves through the water with snake-like body movements.

Coastal Dermatobranchus.

Papillate Armina.

VEILED NUDIBRANCHS

The veiled nudibranchs (or arminaceans) generally have longitudinal ridges running along their back, no visible gills and a fleshy lobe on the head. Species from this suborder are not as common as other nudibranchs, and divers generally have to put in a bit more effort to find them. One species seen throughout New South Wales is the Papillate Armina (*Armina papillata*), which is black with white stripes and often confused with several similarly patterned species. The Papillate Armina is generally found on sandy bottoms as it feeds on sea pens. A smaller undescribed species found in New South Wales and Queensland is the Coastal Dermatobranchus (*Dermatobranchus* sp.).

NUDIBRANCH SECRET WEAPONS

Being very colourful and soft bodied, you would thing that nudibranchs would fall prey to fish and other marine animals. However, very few animals eat nudibranchs as most species are toxic. These colourful sea slugs have developed their dazzling array of colours to warn predators that they are unpalatable and to stay away. These toxins are found in the flesh, and are designed to leave a bad taste in the predator's mouth, so that the nudibranch is spat out and the predator learns to never bite them again. Some nudibranchs develop their

Tubercular nudibranchs eat hydroids and store stinging cells in their cerata.

own toxins, but others absorb them from the food they consume. Nudibranchs are so toxic that many other species mimic their colours to avoid becoming a meal. Species of tubercular nudibranchs have another secret weapon. These creatures feed on hydroids, and can consume their stinging cells, known as nematocysts, without triggering them. They then assimilate these stinging cells into their body, ready to be used for their own defence.

SPANISH DANCER NUDIBRANCH

Most nudibranchs are only a few centimetres long, but one of the most spectacular members of this family is a giant – the beautiful Spanish Dancer (*Hexabranchus sanguineus*). This wonderful sea slug is found throughout the Indo-Pacific region, including in Western Australia, Queensland and northern New South Wales. Reaching a length of 40cm, you would think it would be hard to miss, especially with its pretty red and white colouration. However, Spanish Dancers are far more active at night, so are seldom seen during the day. The species was named after the way it undulates its body while swimming, in a manner reminiscent of a flamenco dancer's dress. The Spanish Dancer is so large that it cannot retract its gills like its relatives, and is often home to hitchhikers, with Imperial Shrimps (*Periclimenes imperator*) living in a commensal relationship on this large nudibranch.

The large and beautiful Spanish Dancer.

NUDIBRANCH MATING GAME

Most mollusc species are rarely seen mating, with the intimate act usually taking place away from prying human eyes. However, nudibranchs are either not shy about sex or doing it all the time, as they are one family of molluscs that are often observed copulating. Nudibranchs are hermaphrodites, and each individual has both male and female sex organs located in the neck. When a pair of nudibranchs of the same species meet, they identify each other by chemoreceptors and body contact. They then position themselves head to tail so that their genital openings align, and insert their penis into the other animal. They can remain joined like this for minutes or days. Once they have fertilised each other they move off to lay their eggs, which are ribbon-like and generally laid next to or on their preferred food. A common nudibranch behaviour, often seen before mating, is tailing, with one animal following the tail of another. Nudibranchs are very short-lived, with most species living less than one year.

A spiral ribbon of nudibranch eggs.

A pair of mating Bennett's Hypselodoris (*Hypselodoris bennetti*).

Mating Red-gilled Nembrotha (*Nembrotha rutilans*).

A pair of Tryon's Risbecia (*Risbecia tryoni*) tailgating.

BIVALVES

Bivalves

The bivalves form the second largest class of molluscs, with more than 9,200 species found in saltwater and freshwater. These molluscs live in two shells, called valves, which are joined at the bottom and open and close around a muscular hinge. Most bivalve shells are bilaterally symmetrical, and these molluscs have no head and no radula teeth, as most are filter-feeders. Bivalves typically rest on the seafloor, either buried in the sand or attached to rocks or some other solid base. They draw water into their shells in order to breathe and feed, trapping plankton and other food particles on modified gills called ctenidia.

The shells of bivalves vary greatly in shape, size and design. Most species are small, less than 10cm long, but the giant clams can be more than one metre wide. This order contains more than 100 families that live in a wide variety of habitats. Most species of bivalves live in a marine environment, and usually in shallow water close to their preferred food. Many bivalves also live in estuaries, or areas with large water movements, as the tides bring them a constant supply of fresh food. Others live in freshwater lakes, rivers and creeks, however some are also found in the deep ocean, especially around hydrothermal vents.

Bivalves vary greatly from other shelled molluscs, and are more primitive than their

Thorny oysters are found in tropical waters.

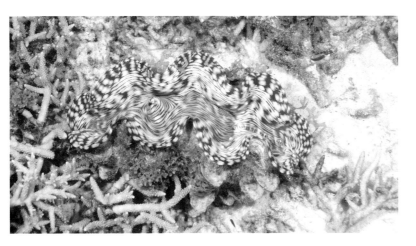

A variety of giant clam species are found in Australia.

gastropod cousins. These creatures have a simple nervous system and no brain. Their sensory organs are also quite simple – some species have basic eyes, but most only have light-sensitive cells. They also have chemoreceptors for taste and touch, which are either located on tentacles or around a siphon used for feeding and breathing.

Within the bivalve shell is the mantle, which encloses the internal organs, and a foot. While most bivalves are fixed to the bottom, there are many species that move around. Most use their foot for mobility, flicking it out of the shell to push the animal across the bottom. They can also use this foot to bury into the sand and mud. The scallops have a more advanced way to get around, as they are able to swim by opening and closing their shell and expelling water.

Reproduction in the bivalves is very simple, especially as many are welded to the bottom. Most species have separate sexes, but a few are hermaphrodites, and they release eggs and sperm into the water simultaneously, triggered by water temperature, time of day or phases of the moon. There are a number of triggers to this spawning which are still not fully understood. A fertilised egg will drift for several days before a larva hatches, settles on the bottom and metamorphoses into its adult form. However, some female bivalves draw in the male's sperm and fertilise the eggs internally, before expelling the larvae.

Humans consume many bivalve species, such as oysters, scallops and mussels, as these molluscs have very succulent meat. While some species are taken from the wild, most of these are farmed in very successful forms of aquaculture. Other species of bivalves have also been collected for their shells, with pearl oysters turned into buttons. This class of molluscs is also famous for producing pearls, which occur very rarely in nature, but are today mass produced thanks to a seeding process.

There are actually five subclasses of bivalves, and many different family groups. This guide book doesn't have space to look at all five subclasses, instead focusing on several families and species from the two largest subclasses that are commonly seen in Australian seas. The largest subclass is pteriomorpha, which contains the mussels, oysters and scallops. Molluscs with this subclass are typically attached to the bottom and have a reduced foot, but a few have broken their bottom attachment. Species within the subclass heterodonta are typically burrowing bivalves, with this group including the cockles, clams and giant clams.

MUSSELS

Mussels are pear-shaped bivalves that are typically found attached to rocks in shallow water. They anchor to rocks by secreting filaments called byssuses, which give the mollusc a solid attachment point to avoid being dislodged by waves. However, some mussel species live on sandy or muddy bottoms and burrow into the substrate.

Mussels are usually found in large colonies, with hundreds and often thousands of shells packed tightly together. A popular seafood, mussels have been consumed by people for thousands of years and today are farmed in very successful aquaculture programs. Mussels are filter-feeders, sucking in water to collect food particles. They don't do well in polluted water, and their flesh can also become poisoned during a 'red tide', when they consume microscopic protozoans. Mussels are consumed by many marine animals, including Eleven-arm Seastars (*Coscinasterias muricata*) in southern Australia.

Mussels are most commonly found in cooler temperate waters, and a number of species occur around Australia. The most common species, and the one most frequently consumed, is the Blue Mussel (*Mytilus galloprovincialis*), which can grow up to 13cm in length but is usually smaller. It is unclear whether this is a native

Blue Mussels are most commonly found in large clusters.

Hairy Mussels are generally found in estuaries.

Old mussel shells are often found washed up on beaches.

Eleven-arm Seastars consume mussels.

species as it is also found in many other countries – it is possible that it arrived in Australian waters attached to a ship's hull, or even in ship ballast water.

One of the most common species found around Australia is the Hairy Mussel (*Trichomya hirsuta*), which grows to 6cm in length and typically has hairy bristles on its shell. It is often found in estuaries, where thick beds of these mussels develop in areas with muddy bottoms.

OYSTERS

Oysters are one of the best-known members of the bivalve family, not only because they are popular to eat, but also as they are commonly seen at low tide on beach rocks. The oyster family is quite large and varied, and in addition to those that attach to rocks many other species live on the seafloor on sandy or muddy bottoms.

Colourful Cock's Comb Oysters attach to corals and rocks.

The Sydney Rock Oyster is farmed for its meat.

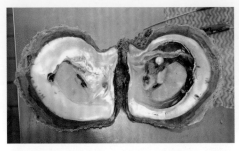

The inside of a farmed South Sea Pearl Oyster shows a cultured pearl.

A South Sea Pearl Oyster.

Oysters have been consumed by people for many thousands of years and were one of the first molluscs to be farmed. They can be consumed cooked or raw, and in Australia oyster farms are more commonly found in southern waters. The most frequently consumed member of this family is the Sydney Rock Oyster (*Saccostrea glomerata*), which is found from southern Queensland to central Western Australia.

While a number of other oyster species that attach to beach rocks can be seen around Australia, the more interesting and colourful members of this family are found underwater, below low tide. Many oyster species attached to corals in tropical waters, including the Cock's Comb Oyster (*Lopha cristagalli*). This distinctive species, with its jagged mouth, can reach a size of 20cm. They are nearly always brightly coloured, as the shell gets covered by encrusting sponges.

The most famous oysters are the ones used to cultivate pearls, with the South Sea Pearl Oyster (*Pinctada maxima*) the most common variety in Australia's tropical waters. This species can grow to 30cm in diameter and normally lives wedged into the sand in areas of large tidal movement. Like many other oysters, the meat of the South Sea Pearl Oyster is also highly prized.

THORNY OYSTERS

Thorny oysters are more closely related to scallops than oysters. This family contains around 50 species that are found in tropical waters and cement themselves to the bottom, much like oysters do. These molluscs are commonly seen in areas where currents occur.

The Giant Thorny Oyster attaches to reef walls.

The most common species seen on the Great Barrier Reef is the Giant Thorny Oyster (*Spondylus varius*), which grows to 25cm in width and is often seen with its shell open and its colourful mantle exposed. Like all thorny oysters it has rows of small blue eyes on its mantle, but is quick to close if a diver gets too close.

SCALLOPS

Coral Scallops burrow into hard corals.

Doughboy Scallops are often found in large groups.

One of the most unusual families of bivalves, as unlike their relatives that are either cemented to rocks or wedged into the sand, most scallops can move about by swimming. Scallops are found throughout the oceans of the world and many species are highly prized for their flesh. In Australia scallops are trawled in Bass Strait, which is not the most environmental friendly fishery as many other species are captured as bycatch.

The flesh of scallops is also eaten by many marine animals, and one of the reasons that these creatures swim, by rapidly opening and closing their shells, is to escape from predators. Swimming scallops are generally found living on sandy bottoms, and often bury in the sand to hide from predators. However, other scallop species live on coral reefs and rocky seafloors and don't swim, instead cementing themselves to the bottom. Scallops have a more developed nervous system compared to other bivalves, and also have rows of eyes on the edge of their mantle.

The classic fan-shaped scallop shell has always been popular with people, being used in jewellery and art, as a religious icon and even in advertising. Shell collectors prize these shells, especially the rarer varieties.

Numerous scallop species are found around Australia in tropical and temperate waters, however these molluscs are far more abundant in cooler seas. One of the most common species seen in southern waters is the Doughboy Scallop (*Chlamys asperrimus*), which can grow to 11cm in width, although most are less than

6cm wide. These colourful scallops are always covered in encrusting sponges, which are thought to make them less palatable to predatory seastars. Doughboy Scallops can swim, but most attach to the bottom using filaments, called byssuses.

In tropical waters scallops are not always seen by divers, as they tend to be on sandy bottoms in shallow murky water. One common species on coral reefs is the Coral Scallop (*Pedum spondyloideum*) – an unusual species that is found burrowed in hard corals and reaches a length of 6cm. While it would appear that the scallop is damaging its coral host, in fact studies have found that the scallops protect their host coral from attacks by the Crown-of-thorns Seastar (*Acanthaster planci*), by expelling water and irritating the seastar until it departs.

FILE SHELLS

File shells are closely related to scallops and have similar shaped shells, but are more likely to be found anchored to the bottom. Around 130 species of file shell have been identified from marine habitats around the planet. Like scallops, some file shells can swim by opening and closing their shell and expelling water, however they rarely swim, as most species live under rocks or shelter under ledges. File shells can

The beautiful Flashing File Shell.

be distinguished from scallops as they have numerous long tentacles protruding from their shell.

While a number of file shell species can be found around Australia, these molluscs are not often observed by divers, as most species are small and remain well hidden. The most commonly seen species is the Flashing File Shell (*Ctenoides ales*), which also happens to be the most spectacular member of the family. This tropical species is also known as the Disco Clam, and these bright red shells can flash bright neon colours across their mantle. These creatures have a reflective tissue that mirrors the ambient light, and the flashing is caused by the animal covering the tissue.They are found throughout the Great Barrier Reef and are highly sought after by underwater photographers, although they tend to hide under ledges and a good guide is often required in order to find them.

COCKLES

The Common Pipi is often sold in seafood shops.

Most Australians are very familiar with cockles, as they are found buried in the wet sand at low tide at beaches around the country. Often dug up to be used as bait by fishers, many people also eat these small molluscs.

The cockle family contains around 200 species. These bivalves typically have a rounded shell that can completely close tight, to retain moisture if the animal is left high and dry at low tide. Cockles don't attach to the bottom, but move with the aid of a foot. These filter-feeders are often found in very shallow water, usually in the surf zone, and bury themselves in the sand as the tide falls, to avoid predators such as sea birds.

While many species of cockles are found around Australia, one of the most common is the Common Pipi (*Plebidonax deltoides*). Also known as the Coorong Cockle, it reaches a length of 8cm, is very widespread, and is collected by commercial and recreational fishers, although stocks have declined in many parts of Australia due to overfishing.

GIANT CLAMS

The largest of all the bivalves are not really part of the clam family, but are actually a variety of cockle. The shells of the largest giant clams grow to more than a metre wide, although the family also contains a few smaller members. Eight species of giant clam are recognised, and they are common throughout the Indo-Pacific Region.

Giant clams anchor to the bottom on shallow reefs. Like other bivalves they are filter-feeders, but they supplement their diet in a very unusual way. The mantle spreads out beyond the shell mouth and is covered in algae, called zooxanthellae, which photosynthesise and provide the clam with additional nitrates, phosphates and carbon dioxide. Giant clams also differ from most bivalves in being hermaphrodites, having both male and female sex organs. They are broadcast spawners, releasing eggs and sperm into the water to be fertilised. To ensure that surrounding giant clams

Giant Clams are common on the Great Barrier Reef.

spawn at the same time they also release a spawn-inducing substance as a trigger.

Giant clams are slow-growing, and may possibly live for more than 100 years. However, many species are threatened from fishing pressures, as their flesh is prized in Asia. Many species of giant clam are found in Australia's tropical seas, including the biggest, which is simply called the Giant Clam (*Tridacna gigas*). It has been reported to grow to 1.7m in width, but the largest confirmed width has been 1.4m. These giant molluscs are quite a sight when viewed close-up underwater, and pose no danger to divers.

PEN SHELLS

Pen shells are closely related to clams, and having very sharp edges they are also known as razor clams. They usually live on sandy or muddy bottoms with only the top half of the shell exposed, so that the mollusc can feed and breathe. Their shells are triangular in shape and usually very thin. Pen shells anchor to rocks buried in the sand with strong filaments called byssuses, which in the past has been used by many cultures to produce clothing. Today they are eaten by many groups of people around the planet.

The most common species found in Australia is the Bicolour Pen Shell (*Pinna bicolor*), which can grow to 50cm in length. It is found almost everywhere except Tasmania, often occurring in large groups in bays and estuaries.

Right: Bicolour Pen Shells are generally found in clusters.

Opposite: A diver inspects an impressive Giant Clam.

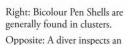

CEPHALOPODS

Cephalopods

This is without doubt the most interesting and varied group of molluscs. The family includes octopus, cuttlefish, squid and nautilus – animals that look nothing like any of their relatives in the very large mollusc family.

Although cephalopods look very different to all other molluscs, they still have many of the same features, including a mantle that encloses their body organs, an armed tongue, and also feather-like gills contained within the mantle for respiration. However, cephalopods differ in having arms that radiate around the mouth and they move by a form of jet propulsion, by funnelling water through a siphon. The differences don't end there, however, as they squirt ink as a form of defence, generally have very good eyesight and most can change the colour and texture of their skin in order to camouflage themselves. Cephalopods are also highly intelligent and have great puzzle-solving skills.

Cephalopods evolved around 500 million years ago, and for many millions of years dominated the oceans of the world until the fish arrived. The first cephalopods lived within a chambered shell, and looked similar to the nautilus of today. Some of these animals were huge, close to 2m in diameter. Over time the cephalopods evolved to avoid being eaten by fish, so most became smaller and either lost the external shell or fused it internally. Today, around 800 species of cephalopods are found around the world, with Australia home to a huge variety of these animals, many of which are endemic.

The Southern White-spot Octopus is only seen at night.

The Bigfin Reef Squid is a tropical species.

A pair of male Giant Cuttlefish battle for the right to mate.

NAUTILUS

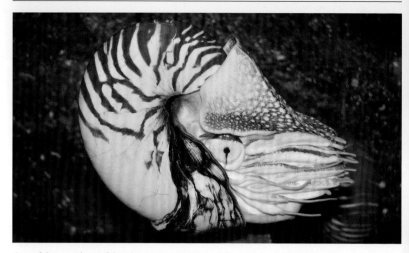

One of the most beautiful and primitive members of the cephalopod family is the Chambered Nautilus.

Still living in an external hard shell, members of this family are the most primitive of the cephalopods. While many species have been extinct for many millions of years, several members still survive in the deep waters of the Indo-Pacific region. The shell of the nautilus is highly prized by collectors, which has resulted in these unique animals declining in numbers due to overfishing. The shell is not only pretty, but very interesting structurally – it contains about 30 chambers, with the animal only living in the last chamber, while the rest are used for buoyancy.

Nautilus have very basic eyes, which are little more than a pin-hole, as they live in deep dark water. These strange animals have around 90 arms that lack suckers, which they use to grab prey, but they are thought to be mainly scavengers. Nautilus live in depths beyond 500m during the day, but rise into shallower water at night to feed.

CHAMBERED NAUTILUS

The most common species in this family is the Chambered Nautilus (*Nautilus pompilius*), which is found throughout the Indo-Pacific Region, including in northern Australia. This creature attains a shell size of around 22cm in diameter and is thought to live for 20 years. They prey mainly on crustaceans, but will feed on any dead animal they can find using the sensory cells on their arms. Like all nautilus they have a hard leathery hood above the head that can be pulled closed to protect the animal from attack.

Nautilus control their buoyancy by adjusting the gas and fluid in the chambers of their shell. Males have four modified arms that deliver sperm into the body cavity of the female during mating. The gravid female then deposits her eggs on the reef and the young hatch between 8–12 months later. Nautilus only mate once a year and don't reach sexual maturity until 15 years old.

DIVING WITH NAUTILUS

Living in deep water, nautilus are creatures that divers rarely see. However, dive charter boats that visit Osprey Reef, 350km north-east of Cairns, Queensland, have found a way for divers to see these amazing animals. Working closely with researchers from the Central Queensland University, overnight the crew lower a baited trap down a coral wall that drops 1km to capture Chambered Nautilus. After the nautilus are measured and studied, divers get to accompany these primitive creatures on their journey back down the wall, until they disappear into the abyss.

CUTTLEFISH

The cuttlefish family is quite large, containing more than 120 species. While most members of the family look very similar in shape, some more closely resemble squid and even have the word 'squid' in their name, such as the bottletail squid, bobtail squid, pygmy squid and the strange ram's horn squid. All cuttlefish have eight arms and two longer feeding tentacles; they use the latter to capture prey, which can include crabs, shrimps and fish. Cuttlefish also have an elongated body that contains a chambered shell known as a cuttlebone, which is used for buoyancy.

Cuttlefish have excellent eyesight, with a W-shaped pupil. They cannot see colour, which is amazing considering the colours these creatures can exhibit to human eyes, but they can observe the polarization of light, which aids their awareness of contrast. Most cuttlefish are active by day, stalking the reef for food. However, a number of species are nocturnal, and spend the day hidden under a layer of sand. It was recently discovered that cuttlefish are venomous, like the blue-ringed octopus, but the toxicity of this venom varies greatly between species.

Mating cuttlefish lock together in a tangle of arms, which allows the male to insert a modified arm into the female's body cavity and deliver a package of sperm. The female may mate with several different males before she fertilises her eggs, which she deposits under rocks or among coral. The female leaves the eggs to develop unguarded, as cuttlefish generally only live for one to two years, and die soon after mating.

Cuttlefish are found in most oceans around the planet, but do not occur off the Americas. They are mostly found in shallow water, although some species prefer deeper water, inhabiting depths to 180m. Australia is home to the world's most diverse cuttlefish fauna, and most species are endemic.

GIANT CUTTLEFISH

Giant Cuttlefish often shelter in caves during the day.

The largest member of the cuttlefish family is found only in the waters off southern Australia and is appropriately called the Giant Cuttlefish (*Sepia apama*). Its mantle grows to a length of 50cm, but with its long arms the animal can be more than a metre long. This species is common on reefs from central New South Wales through southern coasts to central Western Australia, and is regularly encountered by divers. Giant Cuttlefish are often curious of people, and have been known to follow divers around a reef, and even grab cameras and dive gear. Dolphins, sharks, fish and seabirds are known to prey on Giant Cuttlefish.

THE MATING GAMES OF GIANT CUTTLEFISH

The mating habits of Giant Cuttlefish were rarely observed by divers until an aggregation site was discovered off Whyalla, South Australia. Each winter, from May to August, thousands of Giant Cuttlefish gather in the shallow waters here to mate. Large males and smaller females pair up to copulate, however rival males are always on hand to contest for the right to breed. The large males size each other up, and pulsate waves of colours across their bodies. They also flatten their mantle and splay their arms to make themselves look bigger. Eventually the smaller male will back down and swim away, so the animals rarely come to blows.

These cuttlefish are a major tourist attraction at Whyalla and divers come from around the world to see the only mass aggregation of any cuttlefish species. Researchers have also closely studied these mating Giant Cuttlefish and discovered a very interesting aspect of behaviour – cross-dressing males! Researchers have observed smaller males displaying female colours in order to sneak under the guard of the larger males and get close to the females.

A pair of mating Giant Cuttlefish at Whyalla.

Once beside the female they change back to their male colouration and quickly mate, before the larger male becomes aware of the fact that he has been tricked. Researchers also discovered that these cross-dressing males have a higher mating success rate than the larger males!

BROADCLUB CUTTLEFISH

The most common cuttlefish species seen in Australia's tropical waters is the Broadclub Cuttlefish (*Sepia latimanus*), which has a mantle length of up to 40cm long, although they are rarely more than 30cm long. Divers often encounter this species on the Ribbon Reefs, north of Cairns, Queensland. These pretty cuttlefish are wonderful to watch as they silently stalk between the corals looking for food, while divers have also witnessed females gently depositing small round white eggs between the branches of coral. The species is also found throughout South-East Asia, where it is captured for human consumption.

The Broadclub Cuttlefish is a tropical species and often seen on the Great Barrier Reef.

CHAMELEONS OF THE SEA

This Reaper Cuttlefish has changed its colour and skin texture to camouflage with the seafloor.

Cuttlefish are quite intelligent and have a complex communication system involving colour patterns and skin changes. Often called the chameleons of the sea, they can instantaneously change the colour of their skin to either camouflage themselves, dazzle prey or display to other cuttlefish. They can change their colour rapidly because of multiple cell types within the skin known as chromatophores, iridophores and leucophores.

The chromatophores provide the colour, and are cells containing countless colour pigments that the animal can expand and contract to control the colour content. Under these chromatophores are the iridophores and leucophores, which are reflective cells stacked together that mirror iridescent colours. Cuttlefish can control their colour patterns so well that males have been known to display to potential mates with one side of their body while warning off rival males by flashing different patterns on the other side.

These incredible creatures can also change the texture of their skin by controlling muscles. This helps cuttlefish to camouflage themselves from predators, changing their skin texture to lumps and spikes in order to mimic adjacent terrain. Octopus, and squid to a lesser extent, also have this wondrous ability to instantly change their colour and skin texture.

REAPER CUTTLEFISH

Reaper Cuttlefish.

One of the prettiest small cuttlefish found in Australia is the Reaper Cuttlefish (*Sepia mestus*), which is found only on rocky reefs off New South Wales and into southern Queensland, growing to a length of 14cm. While these cuttlefish can change to any colour, they generally display a base colour of red, pink or orange, which makes them a favourite subject for underwater photographers. Reaper Cuttlefish are very common on rocky reefs off Sydney and Port Stephens, and divers often see pairs resting on the bottom.

THE CUTTLEBONE

Unless you enter the water to snorkel or dive, the only part of a cuttlefish that most people see is their internal shell, known as the cuttlebone. Located in the top of the mantle, the cuttlebone is made of aragonite and is riddled with small chambers. Cuttlefish use the bone for buoyancy, which is controlled by the amount of air and liquid pumped into the bone. Each cuttlefish species has a different shaped cuttlebone. Cuttlebones regularly wash up on beaches around Australia and have many uses. Most commonly they are found in the pet trade, for cagebirds to munch as a source of calcium. However, jewellers also use cuttlebones for moulds when casting small pieces of jewellery.

Cuttlebones often wash up on Australian beaches after storms.

This pair of male Mourning Cuttlefish are displaying their best colours to win the right to mate.

MOURNING CUTTLEFISH

Another common small Australian cuttlefish is the wonderful Mourning Cuttlefish (*Sepia plangon*), which grows to a length of 15cm and is found in New South Wales and Queensland. It is usually a sandy brown colour, which helps to camouflage it on sandy seafloors and around seaweeds in its preferred habitat of sheltered bays and estuaries. Divers regularly encounter Mourning Cuttlefish in Sydney Harbour, Botany Bay and Port Stephens, and when breeding it is common to see several males battling each other for the right to mate.

FLAMBOYANT CUTTLEFISH

While many cuttlefish find prey on the seafloor, the Flamboyant Cuttlefish (*Metasepia pfefferi*) spends so much time on the bottom that it has learnt to walk. This small species, which only grows to 8cm in length, uses two arms and two folds on the underside of the mantle to slowly walk across the bottom while searching for prey. They are appropriately named, with their base colour a mix of white, yellow, pink and brown. Flamboyant Cuttlefish are found throughout South-East Asia and in the tropical waters of Australia, although

A lovely Flamboyant Cuttlefish.

they are not common in Australia and are only occasionally seen by divers. Observing them underwater is a real joy as they are generally unconcerned by the presence of divers and continue with their normal behaviour, which can include hunting prey, mating or laying eggs.

SOUTHERN DUMPLING SQUID

Southern Dumpling Squid emerge from the sand at night to feed.

Bobtail squid and bottletail squid are small species of cuttlefish that bury themselves in the sand during the day and emerge at night to feed. These two families of cuttlefish look very similar, both having short stumpy mantles and arms. Bottletail squid generally feed on the bottom, while the bobtail squid swim in the water column to feed, and have a light organ with luminescent bacteria that minimises their silhouette, making them less obvious to predators. Several species of bobtail squid are found in Australian waters, with the most common and widespread being the Southern Dumpling Squid (*Euprymna tasmanica*). These cute little cuttlefish are often seen by divers at night, and are best observed on the sand, as once they enter the water column they are very difficult to see. They grow to 7cm in length and are found in temperate waters from central Western Australia to southern Queensland.

STRIPED PYJAMA SQUID

One of the most spectacular cuttlefish found in southern Australia is the endemic Striped Pyjama Squid (*Sepioloidea lineolate*). A member of the bottletail squid family, these wonderful creatures are white with black stripes and grow to a length of 7cm. Only found off New South Wales, South Australia and southern Western Australia, the Striped Pyjama Squid is a nocturnal species that hides in the sand during the day and emerges at night. A favourite with underwater photographers, it is locally common but sometimes difficult to find, as even at night it will quickly bury in the sand if disturbed.

The Striped Pyjama Squid is one of the most striking members of the cuttlefish family.

SQUID

Squid eggs are generally found in bunches anchored to the bottom.

Squid are very similar to cuttlefish in shape and design, with an elongated mantle, eight arms and two longer feeding tentacles. They also have excellent eyesight, and most species have large eyes. However, squid differ from cuttlefish by having a much reduced internal shell within the mantle, which is little more than a spiny rod and known as a gladius. Similar to cuttlefish and octopus, squid also have chromatophores in their skin that allow them to change colour instantly, but they can't change the texture of their skin like their cephalopod cousins.

Around 300 species of squid are found in the oceans of the world, and while many occur in shallow water, others inhabit dark deep water. Squid are the largest members of the mollusc family, and also the largest invertebrate species. Many species grow to more than one metre in length, but the largest members of the family are the Giant Squid (*Architeuthis dux*) and Colossal Squid (*Mesonychoteuthis hamiltoni*), which grow to at least 14m in length.

Squid live a pelagic life, swimming in the water column, and only come to the bottom to feed and lay eggs. Smaller squid only live for one year, and die soon after mating, while larger species may live for up to five years. Squid reproduce in a similar way to cuttlefish, with the male depositing sperm into the female via a modified arm. The female then lays a clutch of cylinder-shaped eggs, which she attaches to rocks, coral or some other solid structure.

While all cephalopods are captured for human consumption, squid are heavily targeted in fisheries around the world, with the mantle used to make calamari. A number of squid species are found in the waters around Australia, but only two species are commonly encountered by divers and snorkelers.

SOUTHERN CALAMARI SQUID

Found in temperate waters in the southern states of Australia, as its name implies the Southern Calamari Squid (*Sepioteuthis australis*) is a popular target for fishers. Growing to a length of 50cm, they are usually found in small schools of a dozen or so individuals. This species can be seen by day or night, but is far more active after dark when feeding on small fish and crustaceans. They are attracted to light at night, as

Southern Calamari Squid.

is their prey, with fishing boats deploying large banks of lights to attract the squid to their jigs. However, Southern Calamari Squid are also attracted to a diver's torch, so often dance around divers when exploring the underwater world at night.

BIGFIN REEF SQUID

The most common squid species in Australia's tropical waters is the Bigfin Reef Squid (*Sepioteuthis lessoniana*). Growing to a length of 40cm, they are found in depths to

100m, but venture into shallow water at night to feed. This species is common on coral reefs, and is often observed in small schools. Its eggs, which are white fleshy capsules that look like a clump of finger-like sea anemones, are regularly found attached to rocks, coral, mooring ropes and even jetty pylons. Upon closer inspection it is often possible to see the developing young, with their black eyes quite prominent.

Bigfin Reef Squid.

OCTOPUS

One of the most diverse groups of cephalopods, octopus come in a range of different shapes and sizes to suit their environment. They have eight arms and no tentacles, with the underside of each arm covered in rows of suckers that are used to grip prey and other objects. Octopus are very different to other cephalopods – they have no internal shell, and while they can swim, most species prefer to walk, or stalk, across the bottom.

The masters of camouflage, octopus can change the colour and texture of their skin to match their background. Like cuttlefish, they have cells called chromatophores, iridophores and leucophores in their skin which allow them to change to any colour. They also have excellent eyesight, and have been found to be quite intelligent, with a good memory.

Octopus live for between six months and five years depending on the species, and are better parents than other cephalopods. When mating, the male inserts a modified arm into the body cavity of the female to deliver a package of sperm. The female then lays a clutch of eggs in her den, and guards them until they hatch, then she sadly dies.

Around 300 species of octopus are found around the world. Most are bottom-dwellers, but a few live a pelagic lifestyle in the open ocean and never venture into shallow water. Australia is home to a great variety of octopus species, many of which are found nowhere else in the world.

BLUE-LINED OCTOPUS

The Blue-lined Octopus has a very limited range and is mainly seen in New South Wales.

A Southern Blue-ringed Octopus on the lookout for prey.

The most notorious of all the octopus are the venomous species with blue-rings. Australia is home to at least three species of blue-ringed octopus, and a number of human deaths have been attributed to the bites of these small creatures. The Blue-lined Octopus (*Hapalochlaena fasciata*) is the most common member of this family seen in New South Wales and southern Queensland. A nocturnal species with an arm span of up to 20cm, it lives on rocky reefs and in estuaries, and hides under rocks, shells, bottles and other discarded rubbish, emerging at night to feed on fish and crustaceans. Divers occasionally encounter this species, which is a pretty octopus to observe, and fortunately non-aggressive.

SOUTHERN BLUE-RINGED OCTOPUS

A common species in southern waters, being found off Victoria, Tasmania and South Australia, the Southern Blue-ringed Octopus (*Hapalochlaena maculosa*) has an arm span of 15cm. They are common under piers, as there are many places for them to hide in this environment. Like other species of blue-ringed octopus their blue rings are barely visible while the animal is calm, but flash vivid blue when disturbed or alarmed. Blue-ringed octopus toxin is used by the animal to stun prey, and is injected into the victim when they bite. Divers regularly encounter Southern Blue-ringed Octopus at night, and observe them slowly walking across the bottom in search of prey.

BLUE-RINGED ROMANCE

When most octopus mate it is not a very intimate encounter, as usually the male is on one side of a rock and the female on the other, and the only contact is the male's wandering arm reaching around to inseminate the female. However, blue-ringed octopus like to get a little closer for romance, as they have much shorter arms. When a pair come together to mate the male goes on the attack and jumps onto the

A rarely seen event, mating Southern Blue-ringed Octopus.

female's head. Piggy-backing on the female allows the male to insert his modified arm and deliver the sperm. After mating the female takes special care of the eggs – instead of attaching them in a den, she carries them around until they hatch.

HAMMER OCTOPUS

A sandy coloured octopus that spends a lot of time around the sandy seafloor and in areas of seagrass, the Hammer Octopus (*Octopus australis*) is found off New South Wales and southern Queensland and has an arm span of up to 40cm. A nocturnal species, it likes to bury in the sand during the day and emerges at night to feed. Divers often

Hammer Octopus.

encounter it on night dives off Sydney and Port Stephens. This octopus got its unusual name because the male has a hammer-like club on the end of its third right arm, which is used to deliver a package of sperm during mating.

SOUTHERN KEELED OCTOPUS
A very common octopus in Melbourne's Port Phillip Bay, the Southern Keeled Octopus (*Octopus berrima*) is nocturnal and generally hides in the sand during the day, although it will also take up residence in discarded bottles and cans. This octopus has an arm span up to 50cm and is also found off South Australia and Tasmania. It is typically cream to pale brown in colour, and has a skin fold or keel around its head. Divers regularly encounter this species on night dives off Melbourne, where they are often seen stalking across the bottom looking for crabs to eat.

Southern Keeled Octopus.

OCTOPUS DEFENCES
Fish, sharks, rays, dolphins and seals like to eat octopus, so these clever creatures have developed a number of defences to avoid capture. Camouflage is a key component for octopus defence, as many predators rely on vision to find food. However, many other predators use other senses to find prey, so the octopus has a few other tricks up its sleeve. If being attacked, an octopus can squirt out a cloud of ink to annoy and confuse the predator and allow the octopus to escape. Octopus can swim very quickly for short bursts by expelling water through a siphon. Another way octopus escape predators is to sacrifice an arm, similar to the way lizards can

The Mimic Octopus can change its shape to look like many dangerous creatures.

lose a tail. The lost arm continues to move, distracting the predator while the octopus escapes. The Mimic Octopus (*Thaumoctopus mimicus*) has the most bizarre form of defence, as it changes its body shape and pattern to look like dangerous animals such as lionfish and sea snakes. The Mimic Octopus is a rare species in Australia, being found only in the tropical north.

SOUTHERN WHITE-SPOT OCTOPUS
A temperate species that lives in sandy environments, the Southern White-spot Octopus (*Octopus bunurong*) has an arm span of around 40cm and is found off Victoria, Tasmania and South Australia. Typically reddish in colour with white spots,

it rests in the sand during the day and emerges at night to hunt for crustaceans and small fish. Divers often see this species on night dives under piers in South Australia and Victoria.

Southern White-spot Octopus.

DAY OCTOPUS

Found throughout the Indo-West Pacific region and often seen in Australia's tropical north, the Day Octopus (*Octopus cyanea*) is active by day and night and often encountered by divers exploring the Great Barrier Reef, although it is easily missed due to its camouflaged colouration. With an arm span of 2m, this large species is easily identified by the circular spot below the eye. It feeds on crabs, and the den is often littered with the remains of crabs' legs. Day Octopus are sometimes curious of divers, and have been known to observe divers and even reach out an arm to inspect the strange creatures visiting their realm.

Day Octopus.

OCTOPUS ACCOMMODATION

Most octopus species live on the seafloor and inhabit a home, or den. These dens vary depending on the species. Some simply reside in the sand and find a new home each night, while many small species hide in shells, under rocks and even in discarded cans and bottles. However, a number of larger octopus species make a home in caves or ledges, and are very house proud. These octopus go to great lengths to keep their homes tidy, cleaning out sand and the remains of their meals each day. Divers can usually locate octopus dens by the litter of crab shells and broken shellfish in front of a hole. Some octopus block the entrance to their home with rocks, and they often hold the rocks in position with their arms.

The Hammer Octopus usually lives in the sand, but this one has taken up residence in a can.

The Coconut Octopus gathers shells to form a mobile home.

The Coconut Octopus (*Amphioctopus marginatus*), which is found in Australia's tropical waters, even uses tools, and will collect half coconuts and bivalve shells and pull them together around itself as a home. If the octopus finds a good set of shells it will carry them around like a mobile home.

SOUTHERN SAND OCTOPUS

One of the strangest octopus species found in southern Australia is the Southern Sand Octopus (*Octopus kaurna*), which has a very elongated head and, as its name suggests, lives most of its life around sand. Found in Victoria, Tasmania and South Australia, it hides in the sand by day and searches for food by night. This species can reach an arm width of 50cm, but individuals that large are rarely seen. Divers occasionally encounter this bizarre octopus on night dives under piers.

Southern Sand Octopus.

MAORI OCTOPUS

The largest octopus species found in Australia is the impressive Maori Octopus (*Octopus maorum*). Found throughout southern waters, it can have an arm span of more than 3m. It feeds at night on crustaceans, fish and other molluscs, and is also often active during the day. An encounter with a Maori Octopus is always a memorable experience as their size makes them almost as long as a diver.

Maori Octopus.

OCTOPUS ARMS

The eight arms of the octopus are used for walking and grabbing prey, but also have a number of other uses. Arms are used to investigate objects, not only using the sense of touch, but also taste. The suction cups on octopus arms have chemoreceptors that effectively taste what the animal touches. The arms also have tension sensors, so the octopus knows where the arm is and if it is stretched out or retracted. However, the most amazing fact about octopus arms is that the animal can regrow one if it is lost.

The suction caps on octopus arms not only grip objects but can also taste them.

SYDNEY OCTOPUS

A very common species throughout New South Wales, the Sydney Octopus (*Octopus tetricus*) has an arm span of up to 2m, and is easily identified by its white eyes. It is often observed during the day sitting at the entrance to its den, while at night it stalks the reef in search of shellfish and crustaceans, and has also been known to eat other octopus.

Sydney Octopus.

Umbrella Shell laying eggs

Other Natural History titles by Reed New Holland include:

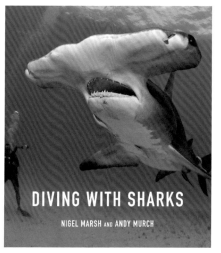

DIVING WITH SHARKS

NIGEL MARSH AND ANDY MURCH

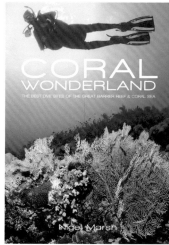

CORAL WONDERLAND

THE BEST DIVE SITES OF THE GREAT BARRIER REEF & CORAL SEA

Nigel Marsh

Nigel Marsh

MUCK DIVING

A Diver's Guide to the Wonderful World of Critters

UNDERWATER AUSTRALIA

The Best Dive Sites Down Under

Nigel Marsh

For details of these and hundreds of other Natural History titles see
www.newhollandpublishers.com

Index